Bleeding Internally Since 1971

Bleeding Internally Since 1971

JASON CHRISTOPHER

bestselling author of The Rogue to Nowhere

RARE BIRD

Los Angeles, Calif.

THIS IS A GENUINE RARE BIRD BOOK

Rare Bird Books
453 South Spring Street, Suite 302
Los Angeles, CA 90013
rarebirdbooks.com

Set in Dante
Printed in the United States

10 9 8 7 6 5 4 3 2 1

Publisher's Cataloging-in-Publication data available upon request.

To my family,
Thank you for having my back when I didn't have a spine.

THE END

HOLLYWOOD CALLED CHECKMATE. I STRUGGLED down Hollywood Boulevard with no clue where I was heading or what I was going to do. And though that had been the theme song of my entire life, the panic and fear hit harder than ever before. The lack of heroin in my system flooded my eyes and left me clueless to my next move. The life I had tried to build for myself was now completely over, and it happened that fuckin' fast. I was more ruined than ever and wasn't sure if it was even worth making it out of this one or not. That was the first time I ever remembered being suicidal.

I started walking toward the Viper Room, the only place that I could think to go. As much of a pain in the ass that I was to everyone in that club, they'd always helped me when I asked for it. And, boy, did I ask for it...

After a few hours of unstable marching beneath the merciless sun, I finally made it to the club. I stood staring at the plastic white doorbell fastened firmly to the stone wall for a good five fucking minutes. This would be the very last time I pushed it.

I had rung that doorbell nearly every morning for the last year, each time looking up into the security camera and doing a little dance or something until someone opened it. Oddly enough, this last morning was almost a year to the day since Ricky had opened the door for me for the very first time. This time there was no dancing, only heavy weeping and a lot of walking sweat, and it would be Tommi, the day manager, opening the door, not Ricky. Her expression was one of curiosity and disappointment as she let my uncontrollably sobbing ass into the club. All I wanted to do was hug her—I needed a hug so fucking badly—but she had already turned around and started walking through the club. I followed her, trying not to stare at her ass, and slumped myself into the chair across from her. I spewed my "woe is me" song, snotting into a handful of bar napkins while she sat behind her desk. Not knowing what to do, and maybe wanting to hand my ass off to someone else, she called Ricky and told him that his fuck up of a little cousin was crying and asking for money to go home.

All throughout the year I had been fucking up left and right—showing up late for work, being too hungover or dope sick or high when I did finally get there—including one time I almost overdosed in Johnny's private room, a big no-no after River's recent passing and contrary to the club's strict new drug policy. So committed were they to the new rule that Sal had once made me kick Blondie's guitar player out for smoking a joint. I was constantly mooching off everyone all the time because I couldn't keep my shit together. Whether it was money, cigarettes, a ride, a place to stay—it just seemed to never end.

Tommi hung up the phone and handed me seventy-five bucks out of the blue money bag in the safe, just enough for a one-way bus ticket back to a shitty existence on the east coast. I was hammering the last nail into my snow-covered coffin having stuffed it full of unattainable dreams.

I took the money, what was left of the stack of napkins, and walked through the club one last time. I dramatically kicked open the Sunset door because I wanted them to see how angry I was about the fact that no one was asking me to stay—like I was some pleasure to keep around. I stared down the street as my tears turned the bright blue sky into a prism, putting a nice farewell rainbow on everything for me...goodbye, Tattoomania, Whisky, Roxy, Rainbow, Panini, Terner's where I would get my smokes and conversation chuckles with Tony every morning...goodbye to all of it. I took one last look into the camera and flipped her off as I started east, toward the bus station.

I took as deep a breath as I could, wishing I could inhale everything and take it all back home with me. I stood on the corner waiting for the light to change with forced visions of Jen pulling up and telling me to get in the car, and we could go back to her place and act like nothing ever happened. Every car that passed me on the road that day looked tiny and red, but none of them were her. I finally arrived at my destination and sat in the parking lot of the bus station biting my nails and huffing bus exhaust for a few hours until mine finally showed up. I gave the dude in the hat my ticket and climbed onto that dingy old Greyhound, planting myself in a seat all the way in the back on a cushion that looked like it had been stained by thousands of ass-cracks that were never wiped properly. I would spend the next two days and twenty-three hours on that piece of shit cushion. Shaking, crying, and negatively analyzing every decision I had ever made. It wouldn't take long before I could see the hole I had just created in my life very clearly, the immediate regret of my actions hit me full-on with no drugs in the way to slow down the rush of intense failure. I was so tired of living. I wanted to drive that bus right off of a cliff, but we were in the desert—so no cliffs.

The only good thing about the rest of this day was that I wasn't going to have to walk around anymore. I was always fucking walking. I was excited to sit there and stare out the window while I rested uneasily into this newfound defeat. I had felt failure many times before, but nothing like this.

The road rash was never going to heal from this crash and, speaking of roads, I was definitely at the end of this one.

The first night on the bus went something like this...

I could either,

A: Pull myself out of the impressively deep hole I had somehow dug for myself and fallen into without even noticing and turn my negative experiences into positive reinforcements using an unstoppable force of positive energy that takes over my soul and allows me to succeed in every endeavor I choose.

Or,

B: I could take the road that would rock me to sleep so hard and fast that if I was lucky, I would never wake up.

I have always felt most comfortable on the path of most resistance.

After about twelve hours into the ride home, all of the skin protecting my body felt like it was peeled back and exposing all the nerves. I was now able to take in the luxurious accommodations of the bloated sardine can I was traveling on. Every time we hit a bump in the road, my spirit would jolt like my tongue was touching a nine-volt battery, and a tiny bit of diarrhea would moisten the outside of my asshole, making me well aware of how fragile I really was.

Quietly, I scowled at the common people in the surrounding seats rummaging through their greased-up brown paper fart bags and crinkling truck stop cheeseburger wrappers as they shoved all day rotator hot dogs stuffed with jalapeño poppers or whatever the fuck into their un-flossed face holes. I rested against the window in the very back next to the bathroom and internally rocked to the septic tank swishing back and forth underneath me, making for a collapsing state of almost-hypnotizing nausea. Every time someone opened the door, Death would rise from the plastic steam hole that was holding everyone's ass blown cancer and singe my eyes while burning out all the hair in my nostrils like a Los Angeles wildfire. I craved to be able to take a deep breath without wanting to vomit in my lap, but I was stuck with all these tuna-sandwich-wrapped-in-tinfoil-eating nobodies. I was nothing like them; I was just like them. I was heading right into the butthole of middle America, and I didn't even have a fucking tuna sandwich. All I had was poor judgement and envy for everyone around me. How were these fucking nobodies able to sit up comfortably and look out the window while they enjoyed their cancer-ridden kibble, while I, the smartest one on the bus, was somehow stricken with this hellfire in my belly? I had a lot to learn about living comfortably in my own body.

I can't decide whether it was more dramatic to say that my organs started to feel like they were being pushed through a pasta maker or a meat grinder—I'll let you guys decide which one might be more painful. All I know is that the entire situation sucked really bad. I couldn't stretch out because the bus was full, so I had to sit there hunched into the corner shaking from the cold sweat and trying not to shit in my pants any more than I already had. I could smell myself, and I wondered if others could too. The only comfort I was able to muster was when I would press my forehead against the window. It was cold, and the only thing that helped, but the vibrations from the engine would rattle the glass, making my nose itch and forcing me to pull away after only a few seconds of pleasure.

I had no money, not a fucking penny in my pocket. I was only able to eat when I could steal from truck stops along the way, a

Snickers bar here, a microwave cheeseburger there, hydrating at every corroded water fountain across America. I only got caught once. One of the managers caught me stuffing a pepperoni Hot Pockets into my pants (cold). He was an unthreatening man in a burgundy vest with dandruff dusting the entire crest of his shoulders. I was so sick and scared that I dropped everything at his feet and ran back to the bus as soon as he confronted me, hoping he wouldn't follow me or tell the bus driver. I was basically surviving by licking the film from my unbrushed teeth. I could feel the lining of my stomach getting thinner as the miles carried on. I was too terrified to steal anything else for the rest of the trip, and I didn't get off the bus until I had to start figuring out a plan for when that bus parked in New York. The ride home made the trip with Jen look like a luxury cruise on the Love Boat with the Rolling Stones. I wouldn't wish that kind of hell on my worst enemy.

THE PICK UP

ANNA AND I STARTED SNORTING heroin together when we lived in Albany with Scott and Kelly, not too long before I left for LA. Nothing too crazy, just a little bit here and there. Maybe when Scott and Kelly were back in Woodstock for the weekend we would find the local crack dealer and spend the night smoking it out of their weed bongs. I knew that both of our habits had progressed during the year I was gone and that there was a good possibility that I could persuade her to load up a couple of syringes and meet me at the bus stop in Newark. I picked Newark instead of NY because it was something like forty-five minutes closer, and after some persistent collect calling, she finally agreed to do it.

Poor Anna. The more minutes that passed on that giant metal tube of suck, the sicker I would get, and the more I would call her crying from every stop we made to make sure that she was still coming.

I was hurling myself right back into what I couldn't escape from fast enough almost a year before to the fucking day. All I had was what I was wearing: a navy blue hoody with bleach and bloodstains up and down the sleeves, an oversized pair of blue carpenter jeans with that dumb denim hammer loop on the side of the leg, and high-top purple Chuck Taylors with dirty white laces.

I was about to enter one of the most brutal winters New York has ever seen.

I was getting home just in time for the blizzard of '96...

After an agonizing three days, we crept into the Newark terminal, and by crept I mean that it took so long to come to a stop I almost kicked the back window out and jumped onto the asphalt. I hustled down the aisle to the front of the bus before it came to a stop so I could be the first one out and pushed my way through the heavy glass doors of the station to where Anna was waiting for me out front. I hadn't eaten in two days and the smell of Newark wasn't doing my stomach any favors, but I wasn't even thinking about food. I just needed to get in the car and stick that needle in my arm real quick so everything could be okay.

As I approached the car, I noticed someone in the passenger seat. She'd brought one of our normal friends down with her for the ride; the kind of friend that you had to be discreet with the dope around. Why the fuck would you do that to me, Anna? I was not happy about this at all. Every piece of cartilage connecting my bones ached, I couldn't swallow, and I needed to get well. I needed to get well right fucking now, in the car. It's all I had been fantasizing about the entire trip.

I got into the back seat all mad as she slipped the syringes into my sweaty palm from the side of her seat, and nobody said a word as we sped off to the nearest public bathroom. Anna knew that this had to happen fast or I was going to lose my mind and blow her cover. I didn't really give a fuck who knew what about me at that point in my life. Everyone knew we were fucking junkies, it was always the pink elephant in the room, but we still had to lie about it and pretend nothing was going on so our normal friends could feel less guilty about hanging out with us.

I made her pull into a Barnes and Noble as soon as we got on the highway, returning to the car fifteen minutes later with a large hot coffee with six sugars and lots of cream, and a vegetable oil-saturated blueberry muffin acting like I hadn't just been shaking, sweating, and completely silent the entire ride to the store. I was upright, walking confidently, and finally able to take deep breaths into my lungs. You know, like a completely normal person does every minute of their life. I have wasted serious amounts of energy for as long as I can remember just to feel like a regular human.

I was finally able to stretch my legs out in the back seat while I itched my nose and name-dropped the fuck out of story after story the entire ride home. I think it was home I was going back to anyway. It felt like it was. I was so over trying to "make it" in LA, so this had to be home. I felt like I had to force myself to be okay with what was happening or I would surely end my life. Besides, I hadn't laughed or felt a sense of comfort like I did in that car the entire time I was in Hollywood. No wonder I felt like such a lonely piece of shit while I was out there. This whole thing was so fucking crazy that it didn't even feel like it had happened, a giant blur out of the longest dream ever. Exhaust crusted snowbanks lined both sides of the thruway as we kept it a steady fifty-five, and even though my soul was completely destroyed, I was relieved that I wasn't going to have to try and support myself anymore. Everyone back home had always enabled me, so I could just do whatever the fuck I wanted. They all really understood what a lazy junky piece of shit I can be, and they were completely okay with it. Not many people can do that.

I got dropped off on the green where I bounced around from couch to couch trying to get my bearings. That didn't seem to be working out, so a few days later she picked me up and took me to a hauntingly gorgeous stone cottage just down the road outside of town. A place set back from the main road just far enough in a tiny canyon to make it the perfect hideout for someone who didn't want to be seen.

I didn't even see the driveway we turned into, all of a sudden we just made this sharp turn and started sliding down a dirt driveway that was slicked over with ice. I was immediately drawn to the chimney on the roof, a bunch of stones cemented together, that was sticking out of what may as well have been giant slabs of gingerbread covered with gobs of vanilla frosting and sprinkled with powdered sugar, the oyster-colored smoke discharged into a somber sky lofting soot over the branches of all the empty trees that surrounded the house. I was so high that it felt like I was seven years old and it was about to be Christmas morning. As I stepped out of the car I was slapped with that old familiar smell of burning winter that I had tried so hard to escape most of my life. The tips of my fingers became instantly numb as I slow danced alone on the iced driveway blowing into my balled-up hands and waiting for Anna to get her shit together so we could walk over and knock on the door.

The house belonged to K, the mother of a beautiful, sweet, young friend of ours who had passed away in a very unfortunate drunk driving accident. I had never met her except for paying my respects at the funeral a few years prior. Somewhere along the path of mourning, K got strung out on pills that were supposed to be helping her cope with this tragic event and either really wanted to try heroin or was already doing it and just needed more—this part of my life is super fogged up, so bear with me as I attempt to piece it all together for us.

Anna brought me over because I still had a couple of local connections that no one else really knew about, and she also figured I would fit right in with their little junky sewing circle. I do remember that just about everyone back home was still snorting it, and that I had forgotten what that was like. Anna was right about K and I getting along, though. We got high, smoked cigarettes, and told stories until pretty late into the evening, and it was the first time I felt like I was home since I'd been back. I slept over that night and basically never left.

I was so embarrassed about coming home that I didn't tell anyone except the people that absolutely needed to know—Anna, whoever had dope, and now K. I did absolutely nothing for weeks but get high, hate myself, and leave despairingly pathetic messages on Jen's answering machine while I laid on the couch sipping decaffeinated tea and eating Stouffer's microwave mac 'n' cheese.

K worked at the hardware store in town and every morning before she left for work she would toss a few bags of the devil's dandruff on the coffee table to get me through the day. I would wake up, shoot up, turn on a shitty talk show, and spend the rest of the day peeking through the curtains of the window behind me every time a leaf rustled in the yard. I would brush short white hairs off of me all day from petting her neurotic, cold-nosed dalmatian until she came home from work with money so I could take the car and get more dope. I was so stoked to have the China white back in my life and could have easily started snorting it again like everyone else, but I had graduated to infected abscesses, cotton fever, and extremely low standards while I was in LA.

It was just K and me most of the time. Sometimes Anna would come over after work to get high before she went home for the night, but for the most part in the beginning it was just us. I'm not sure if I was the one who turned everyone on to the needle or if they were doing it before I got home, I just know that once everyone got on board with that shit it started to get real fucking weird...but also really fucking awesome. I had *always* been the only junky in the room that was using a syringe, and it was *always* an uncomfortable scene. The snorting junkies acted like they were better than you. I know I did when I was snorting.

Actually, I take that back.

The junkies that smoked it (a.k.a. wasted it) were the worst with that shit.

Fuck them, pussies.

Things quickly turned into a bloodbath free-for-all with bleach squirts and bloodstains over everyone's pants and shirts. It was nice not being the only one now, but that also meant that everyone's habits tripled pretty much overnight. The dope started going quicker than it came, and sometimes I would wake up to no baggies on the table, meaning I'd have to sweat and shake until someone went all the way down to the city, copped, and came all the way back, and who the fuck knew when that would be and how long it would take. There weren't many people willing to take that ride because it was so risky. Sometimes it would take a few days to get things rolling again, and oh how fucking brutal that would be.

It's weird when you get dope sick. Your entire makeup changes—the mental and the physical. I could Google some shit right now and try to impress you with smarty-pants stuff, but all I really need to describe is the blanket on the couch. It was so soft and warm and always smelled like fabric softener when I was high, but when I was sick it was rough and scratchy and smelled like a dog that needed a bath. And there were fleas all over it. The air was pungent and nauseating, the dog's nose would brush against my arm or something while I was sweating all over the cold furniture and throw me into a goose-bumped panic.

This little hippy dude had been flying back and forth to Pakistan and supplying most of the town for a couple of years, but I was never able to go to him. I was only able to get it from this complete pile of shit named Cubby. Cubby was a middle-aged, failed-at-life junky with pasty white skin whose hair may as well have been a strip of Velcro glued around a completely bald liver-spotted head. My fondest memory of this scumbag was when I was dying sick on the green and he just stood there licking this vanilla ice cream cone like it was the only piece of pussy he'd ever had in his life, and it probably was, and he was telling me that he was out and didn't have anything. No one is that calm when they don't have anything. Never. I don't know why I keep this memory of that piece of shit so fresh on my brain, but I guess certain things just remind me of why I stay away from all that crap nowadays. I hated having to deal with this guy all the time. If he wasn't on the green, I would have to race over to his shitty apartment outside of town while on a delivery for the fruit stand I was working at in their broken ass delivery van. I was always in a hurry and he never answered his fucking door because he was so high. The flophouse this fool lived in smelled like dead deer and was always a hundred degrees inside. I fucking hated going there. The walk-up had garbage piled on either side all the way to the top, and when he did finally answer, he would be standing there drooling and mumbling in some shit-stained tighty-whiteys and no shirt. The pungent smell festered mainly in his room, so when he opened the door I would get this hot waft of vinegar and dead animal that almost made me puke in my mouth, then I would have to go inside of that fucking room and not be able to leave until he was finally able to get his shit together enough to sell me a bag. A normal junky would have just kicked his door in and stolen it, but he was my only connection at the time, so I had to kid-glove the situation constantly. Getting high was the hardest job I ever had in my life, and I've had some super shitty hard jobs.

Growing up, my family had a tiny pear tree by our pool, and every summer when the pears would sprout or whatever the fuck they do, my grandmother would take a bushel to the fruit stand at the end of our road and trade some greens to cook for our dysfunctional family dinners. I worked there when I was twelve. My oldest and dearest friend Scotty (the one I got stoned with for the first time in book one) worked at Taco Juan's taco stand that was set up in the corner of the parking lot before that, and the place has been a staple in my family since before I was born, so when it came time for me to try and start paying for some of my own stuff as a twenty-five-year-old man, I decided that this was where I would go to seek employment. Matthew, the owner's son, was now running the place and stoked to have me back. Matt was the first guy to smoke weed with me when I was a kid, but that's another story for another book. It was about to be summertime, and that is when business thrives in that town, so they were going to be busy. I started pretty much immediately and worked almost every day, stealing just enough money out of the old-timey register to support my delivery runs to Cubby's. I felt terrible about stealing from them because I didn't want to be a junky thief, and they were always like family, but I also wasn't getting paid enough to get high every day like I wanted to, so I had no choice but to become a junky thief.

Between Cubby and a few other nickel-and-dime scumbags in and around town, the dope was on a pretty regular flow with not too many hiccups straight through the fall. Work was going okay, and I was still at K's though now looking for my own spot. During this time we got wind that George had returned home and was holding court in one of the detox wards in Kingston. I was glad he was back, even though I was still a little mad because the girls in Venice had told me he broke into their apartment when he was homeless on the beach and pawned my guitar.

Anna and I had told K all about George because we knew he was inevitably going to end up at the house; it was only a matter of time. So we basically sat there waiting for him to bust out of treatment and show up at her door. I think Anna or someone had been in contact with him and somehow steered him in our direction, but it definitely wasn't me. It was starting to get bad enough that I would think about getting clean from time to time, so I was excited to hear about detox and how relaxing and helpful it could be.

A few days had gone by and I started to wonder if George was actually going to stay in treatment. I was surprised I hadn't seen him yet and was worried that I was going to be stuck being the low man on the junky pole. Being homeless on Venice Beach had put him one strike below me in my book of wonder. And just as that thought passed through my skull, I heard a car come down the driveway, I peeped out the curtain of the front door window and saw a red station wagon with a magnetic sign on the door that read "KINGSTON TAXI."

I almost died when I saw George step out wearing nothing but a detox robe and those little Totes slippers with the traction on the feet, and a plastic bag that may as well have been tied to the end of a stick. I stared through that little glass diamond feeling my blood speed up into my body; it was fucking on now, boys and girls. As he looked up and gave me the biggest shit-eating grin I had ever seen in my life, and I saw that he was missing one of his front teeth. I dropped dead on the floor laughing before I opened the door and hugged that motherfucker so hard I almost broke our spines. The rhythm section was back, and my blood was pumping for it. Between George, Anna, and me, this junky trifecta roadshow was now ready to hit primetime.

THE RISK...

WE HAD A GOOD thing going now that George was back because he had the in with the hippy dude, so I didn't have to smell Cubby's fucking dirty wet sock of an apartment anymore. Unfortunately, and just our luck, the hippy dude got busted coming back at the airport, thus leaving a sudden and massive hole in the junky community. I didn't even realize how many of the other nickel-and-dime scumbags were getting their shit from him and stepping all over it until he disappeared. There was no dope to be found anywhere. I saw Cubby freaking out on the green trying to find someone to go to the city for him, but nobody would pay attention to him, and that brought me such joy.

Luckily K always had a little stash of Xanax that we could crush up and snort on these unfortunate occasions until someone went and copped. It wouldn't relieve our sickness, but at least we wouldn't have anxiety about being sick. Of course, I tried to shoot them up first, but I just ended up licking it all off the spoon and the syringe because Xanax doesn't break down in the water. Woodstock was scarce again, and we had to do something. We were always waiting on these fucking asshole junkies, and I was getting so tired of it. Over time, K's house became the meeting place where everyone came to get high. With its wood-burning stove, a big screen TV, and decaf teas and blueberry muffins, it was the quaintest little shooting gallery you ever did see.

It got so bad that we actually had to go down and cop ourselves, and that's when we figured out that driving down ourselves to get the drugs would be much more lucrative. Taking a high risk of getting arrested was something I definitely wasn't into, but not having to wait for anyone to bring me overpriced, watered-down dope really lessened that fear. Taking on this task also meant that we would be the ones in control of the people, and we could charge them double what we were paying, which would make all of our dope free. This was a great plan.

I now had a purpose in life a couple of times a week. It was great to have something to look forward to. The new schedule went something like this: I would wake up to the sound of Anna's car pulling down the driveway and immediately put the clothes that were lying on the floor next to the couch back on. Then, if I wasn't too sick, I would crawl to the bathroom and brush my teeth. We would drive to where K worked, and I would run up the back stairs to her office, where she would hand me a wad of cash and the keys to her jeep. Anna and I would switch cars and very carefully, and usually very dope-sick, take the thruway all the way down to Spanish Harlem. It was always either me or Anna hunched over the steering wheel while George or whoever else we picked up and threw in the back seat would play DJ from over the middle console. Alice In Chains' *Dirt* was still fresh on the CD circuit for us "wishin' we were from Seattle" motherfuckers. Crystal Method's first album was also a good one to cruise to. Staring down the middle of the road at those cut yellow lines that were blurred from complex comfortability, waiting so impatiently for a sign, any sign, that we were getting closer to the city to make us feel just a little less sick—oof!

Finally, after hours of holding in explosive diarrhea and suicidal thoughts, we would come around the bend where the George Washington Bridge peaked over the tops of the trees letting us know that we were just about there and everything was probably going to be okay. Almost immediately everyone that had been moaning, groaning, and squirming would bounce up straight and start smiling, laughing, and dancing in their seats. It was like the hand of God himself had cracked through that dingy New York skyline and rested the tips of his old white racist fingers on our clammy foreheads curing us of all worry and sickness.

No one believes that a want is a need more than a junky.

As soon as we crossed over the bridge and got onto the West Side Highway, our speed would increase rapidly not only to keep up with the pace of the angry New York people who really needed to get somewhere because they were so important, but because the dope was so close we could smell it. We would pull over a block or two away from the actual cop spot, and I would be out on the street running before the jeep came to a complete stop. The only white dude on the block and a prime target for dealers, I would put on a fake limp and pull my hoody over my head to cover my bleached yellow hair and infected eyebrow ring in case the cops did a slow cruise past looking for white junkies to harass. I thought the limp made me tough...I would sweep down the block past all the dealers pretending I was some badass while my heart took a shit into my stomach every step of the way. They all shouted the brand name stamped on the wax baggies they were holding in their hands, and I wouldn't stop for anyone until I heard the brand I was looking for. We'd heard through the dope-vine that a bunch of people overdosed and died on some stuff called "Knockout," so I waited until I heard that word and then followed whoever said it into a stairwell that reeked of urine and hot garbage, handed him all my money, and skipped back up the street with the lifeblood placed firmly in my hand, but not too firm that my sweaty palms would destroy it. I just had to be ready to toss it if I suddenly got thrown against a wall. Those cops were fucking stealth up there.

The rule was that no one was allowed to fuck with the dope until we got over the bridge and onto the parkway. The city was extremely hot back then, especially the areas we were copping in. The one time that I was too sick to wait and started to wrap the seat belt around my arm, we got stuck at a light and there was a cop standing on the corner staring right at me, so we had to run the light and barrel down the street hoping he didn't chase us—which he didn't, thank God. After that, we decided that we would wait until we got to the first exit off the parkway and get high in the Dunkin' Donuts bathroom, which we conveniently renamed "Dope 'n' Donuts."

The bathroom in this shithole made the port authority one look like a bed and breakfast on a back road in Connecticut. I ran through all the doors finally getting to an empty toilet and slammed my ass down onto a piss covered seat with my pants still on, sticking the rig right between my legs into the dark yellow toilet water. I didn't give a shit about anything but getting that fairy dust into my pipeline, obviously. It's a miracle I didn't contract sepsis. Shooting up in that bathroom was not only hygienically risky, there were also spaces between the stalls that you could see right through, so if you looked hard enough you could totally see what was going on, and if a cop came in and decided to do the sneaky peak, you were fucking toast. I would strut into the store starving and sweating profusely. I would pull a few napkins from the dispenser and wipe my forehead while I ordered a large light 'n' sweet, a toasted coconut, and two jellies for the ride back. I did this every time we were there, and even today if I find myself in a D&D, I will order the same fucking thing like an eight-year-old.

The car was now fully loaded, and so were we. As we slowly and safely made our way back, I would hang my head out the window, letting the breeze take my head all up into the fresh country air. I was high, and it didn't matter what season it was. There was no hot or cold, only high. My bones were no longer brittle, my ice-cold blood wasn't clogging my pores shut anymore. I was alive again and finally able to enjoy the absolute nothing that my life had become, deep breath after deep, clueless breath.

Somewhere during all of this darkness, Scott and Kelly decided to get married. Anna and I were to be the best man and maid of honor. We were so fucking strung out that Anna had to put makeup on her track marks because the dresses weren't long-sleeved, and I had to leave early because I didn't bring enough dope and got sick. I bounced immediately after the shitty toast I made to his entire family. I will never forget the puzzled look on his father's face because it was so short. Every once in a while that wedding picture pops up and I feel like the biggest piece of shit in the world. At the time I literally had no idea I was doing anything wrong.

After running the game ourselves for a few months, this guy Richie that lived around the corner from K took over the reins and became our main supplier. K just funded his runs now instead of us having to go, which was great because he was pretty consistent for a while. We would still have to wait sometimes, but never for more than a full day, he was just a slow old junky in his sixties. This was pre–cell phone era, so we had to wait until he got all the way back from the city, pulled into his driveway, got out of the car, walked up to the door, looked for the house key, opened the screen, put the key in the lock, turned the lock, reached down to the door handle, turned the handle, pushed open the door, stepped into the kitchen, walked to the phone on the wall, picked up the receiver, dialed our number from a landline, (a landline is a phone that stays in your house), let the phone ring until the answering machine picked up, and wait to see if it was finally him leaving a message. Then, and only then, could we go pick up the drugs. When you are sick and waiting for heroin, every second feels like four minutes.

Sometimes he would take so long to get back we would think he got busted or had a heart attack, but he always came through, and that phone would always ring. We would hover around that fucking answering machine and as soon as we heard his voice after the beep I would fly out the door, rip up the driveway, and race around the corner to his house, stopping at the foot of the driveway to creep in as quietly as I could because of his paranoid ass, and softly knocking on the door awaiting to enter his disgusting, overly heated apartment that had the face punching odor of sour milk and dirty diapers.

One time I walked in and his naked, screaming, somewhere around two-year-old baby that was covered in filth was kicking little orange syringe caps across the living room as his junky mother, carrying a heavy resemblance to Mother Firefly, chased him across the living room. There's no way this kid is not dead or sitting in prison right now. I would grab the dope and speed back to K's and we would all be in the days of wine and roses for at least a day or two before it would start all over again. There was never a solid week of calm, and this is when the detoxes started to come in handy.

DETOX AND THE ABSCESS OF FEAR

SHONDA HAD JUST GOTTEN out of detox and came by the house to see George. I hadn't seen her in years, but she was still smoking hot. I was definitely surprised to see her. Shonda was my first real crush when I was twelve, and we've always had a "thing," even though we have only ever gotten physical with each other one or two times. She had been George's on-again, off-again Wiccan-wife-girlfriend whatever for I don't even know how long, so I tried to keep it in my pants. George and I have always had a little rift with a girl or two that made our relationship untrustable at best, Shonda being one of the two. As we were sitting on the couch catching up—and shooting up—she was telling me how nice it was to have just taken a break from it all, how it had given her veins a rest and whatnot. This got me thinking hard. I didn't know you could take breaks from being a junky, and God knows I fucking needed one. The more thought that went into getting clean, the harder it became to make sense of this life I had come back to.

I think my very first detox was Benedictine Hospital in Kingston. I never lasted more than two days in any of them, so it's hard to keep track, but I do remember two major things about my first institution: The graveyard shift nurse who did my intake said that he wanted to see me fill a plastic cup up with water and drink it every time I walked past his station, and that I should eat bananas because they are the perfect food. Out of all the detoxes and rehabs I have been to in my life, that's literally the only thing that has really stuck with me.

Back in the day, all you needed to do was walk into an emergency room and tell them you needed detox and they had to admit you. If they didn't and something happened to you after you left, you could sue them. When I found out about this, I started going all the time. I would run out of dope or hustle or whatever and convince myself that it was time to finally get clean for real. I was always high when I made this decision. I would tell myself and everyone that would listen that I was going to detox and that this was it, I was done for good. I would break the tips off of all my syringes and throw them in the trash and give all my cottons and scrapers to George or whomever. Now, either two things would happen: I would go into detox that night when I was still high, waking up in a panic the next morning and making K or Anna come pick me up, or I would talk about going all night, but wake up the next morning a little sniffly and canceling the plan until maybe the next day—but tomorrow rarely came.

If I woke up and there were orange pills on the coffee table, it meant Woodstock was dry and I would have to go under the couch cushions for the cottons and scrapers I had stored there for a rainy day. Unfortunately, along with that came a bunch of short white dog hairs and linty type stuff. I would rip the baggies open and scrape the insides clean with a razor blade, swirling all of this mystery together into a spoon full of hot water, dig in my veins for a few minutes with a dull ass needle, and quickly shoot it into my right arm, dog hair and all, hoping to be a little less sick than I was when I woke up. I would do this two or three times with the same spoon, resoaking the used cottons with blood just to make sure I didn't miss anything.

This procedure NEVER worked, and I would always end up trying to shoot the Xanax, gagging as my failed attempt left me licking the spoon. I would sit on the couch sick as fuck, but with no anxiety about it. One morning I woke up to some slight swelling and a weird pain in my right arm, not a lot of pain, but enough to make me realize that something might be seriously wrong.

Back then, the rule was that if you left detox AMA, you couldn't come back for thirty days. Unfortunately, I didn't know that this was a rule until I went to the hospital to get my arm checked out and they told me that I needed to spend the night on an antibiotic IV drip. I had an abscess, and it was infected. Yes, that's right, an infection inside of an infection. Some super junky shit. I told them that if I was to be spending the night in their facility, that I would definitely need to be put into detox and on some sort of medication. They looked at my file and denied me access because I had left AMA a week prior. I had no choice but to tell them to fuck off and once again called K to come and get me.

As I waited outside the emergency room a young doctor just a little older than me in a long white coat came out and literally begged me to stay, telling me that the infection in my arm was going to spread to my chest and into my heart killing me within the next day or so. I asked him one last time to put me in detox, and as he was telling me how his hands were legally tied and that he couldn't, K and George pulled around the bend. I jumped in the back of the Pathfinder and had a needle in my arm before we were even out of the parking lot. I got back to the house and had to have someone else shoot me up all night in my other arm because the one I usually shot up in was too swollen to find a vein. I woke up the next morning with chest pain, skipping heart beats, and an arm the size of my thigh. I had to go back to the hospital and beg them to put me in detox, which they finally decided to do. But the funny part is that it didn't even fucking matter. If you weren't on the methadone program, they didn't give you any good drugs. If you were lucky you got a giant yellow "sleeping pill" that did absolutely nothing but make you groggy and sick.

I spent all that day and most of the night hooked up to an IV. I went in high but eventually started to feel a little cold and shaky, but not that sick yet, and was actually thinking to myself that I might just stick around this shithole hospital and kick the habit once and for all. Morning came and the bag I was hooked up to was empty and the swelling had gone down by at least half. I was a little sick but more relieved that I wasn't going to die. They put me in a wheelchair and took me down to get some x-rays, the nurse stopped in front of the room and walked away for a second, leaving me alone to stare at the automatic door that led out to the free world. For no reason other than pure junky impulse, I jumped out of the chair and ran down the hall, busting through the doors like I was escaping from prison. No one gave a shit, or tried to stop me. I wasn't mandated there. I could have just told the nurse I was leaving and there wouldn't have been a fucking thing she could have done except try to talk me into staying.

Here's how every day was starting to go:

I would wake up in the morning fed up with how my life had turned out, break all my rigs, and have someone drop me off at detox. I would be okay for the night, taking years off my life in the smoke room, but would always wake up sick and call K collect to come get me, or I'd walk out of the hospital to hitchhike back to wherever I was staying. Then I'd find the buried syringes and try to fix them by melting down the tips to get a little bit of the needle to poke through the hard melted plastic so I could dig around into my skin hoping to hit a vein. I think this actually only worked once out of the two hundred times I tried it.

I had probably kicked it on Scott and Kelly's couch or at the foot of their bed on the rug about twenty-five times by now, and they were completely over me stealing all their laundry quarters and sweating all over their two small children. K was literally the only person I had left.

I don't remember how I got back to Woodstock, but when I got back to K's there was a message on the answering machine from my Aunt Marie in New Jersey. This was my father's sister, so I called back curious to see who may have died and secretly hoping it was my father, because it was the only reason I could think of why she would be calling. Turns out it was my grandmother's eightieth birthday and they were throwing a family reunion/birthday party at the VFW hall down the street from her house the next weekend. Everyone was flying in from everywhere and Aunt Marie wanted me to be the surprise. I hadn't spoken to any of these people since I was sixteen years old, back when Grandma and I got into a fight about my dad, who's always been a very touchy subject with me. Listening to the message, I started to remember how her and my grandfather basically raised me every weekend and summer that I didn't go up to Woodstock, and I decided I would go.

THE NO-NO SQUARE

THE SWELLING IN MY arm had gone just about all the way down, except for this one little part in the pit of my arm that had morphed into what I can only describe as a limp pinky finger that hung off my arm like a ginormous skin tag. I tried to hide it when I went back for the reunion and stopped off to see some friends I had grown up with that had no idea what it was like to be a junky, but it was way too hot to wear long sleeves, so I just told everyone I got stung by a giant wasp.

Aunt Marie's house was where Grandma used to take me swimming. Afterward, we would stay for dinner. Uncle Bob was a truck driver and rarely ever home, but when he was, his big burly ass was laid out in front of the television. I'd sit there and watch the buttons sewn in his flannel hold on for dear life as his big belly poked out the bottom and rubbed against the carpet while he snored himself in and out of rug slumber. The dining room furniture was Viking-esque, giant wooden chairs with emblems carved at the top were placed heavily over a mustard-colored rug that went to every corner of the house. My cousin Bobby was strung out at the time and never home. I only remember seeing him once or twice as a child, but his sister Robyn was always there, and I looked forward to seeing her very much when I was younger. She was my hot older cousin who would show me off to her friends because I could name any classic rock song that came on the radio and the band that was playing it, though I guess back then they were just "rock" songs.

One night I ended up spending the night there and slept in Robyn's bedroom, which was up in the attic. We were on the floor lying next to each other on top of open sleeping bags like we were camping while watching *Saturday Night Live*. I remember Bill Murray was screaming that it burned when he peed in a stall while the person next to him told him he had gonorrhea. The next thing I knew I felt my cousin's fingers moving quickly up the side of my thigh in a finger walking motion, and before I knew what was happening, her hand was on my special purpose. I was nine or ten years old, and I can't find that skit anywhere on the internet.

Even with my sexually advanced makeup, I was still way too young to know what was going on. I just knew that whatever she was doing was making my heart beat really fast. She started touching me in places a ten-year-old should never be touched, then taking my tiny, virgin hand, and placing it where a ten-year-old boy's hand definitely shouldn't be, especially on a fourteen-year-old girl. I had no fucking clue what was happening, and she was kind of hot back then, so I didn't really think it was wrong until she told me not to say anything to anyone about it. It was the first of two times that this would happen—this one time in her room, and then once in Grandma Agnes's basement.

What's that? You say you want to read that story, too?

Well, all righty then.

Grandpa died a slow painful lung cancerous death right before my eyes, but all of his things were still untouched in the basement, where I would play to make me feel like he was still there. Pictures of Joe DiMaggio and the Yankees hung all over the cheap wood panel wall surrounding his work desk, the white picture borders aged to the color of a dark yellow and were barely held on by some old Scotch Tape, every picture bent with dryness at the corners. Robyn pulled out the metal chair with red vinyl cushioning propped under the desk and whispered for me to stand on it. I thought we were going downstairs to play but figured she had other plans when she pressed her index finger against her full pink lips and told me to not make a sound as I got up onto the chair. She then began to unzip my Wranglers, eventually pulling them all the way down and flipping my tiny hairless penis out of my Aquaman Underoos. I stood there flaccid, clueless, and quite possibly a little turned on with my hands secured firmly on my hips. She put it in her mouth and started sucking, I watched it stretch back and forth as she pulled on it with her mouth trying to make me hard, but I literally felt nothing—like I might not have been into girls. It turns out I was just ten years old and more interested in burning the heads off of my G.I. Joes.

When I didn't get hard, she pulled down her black stretchy pants and showed me her vageen, like that was going to change everything and turn me on. She started to spread her pussy lips apart telling me to look, and when I turned my tightly closed eyes toward that pubic mountain of junior high madness, all it reminded me of was a grilled cheese sandwich. It's a wonder that I'm not gay.

Just then Aunt Marie opened the door at the top of the stairs yelling down and asking us what the hell we were doing and why it was so quiet. Robyn hurriedly pulled up her underwear, whisper yelling at me to pull up mine as well, and that was that. We both ran upstairs and it was never spoken of again.

Anyway, that's the end of molestation stories for now.

JOE AND THE REUNION

So THERE I WAS IN Aunt Marie's house getting hammered in the basement with Bobby and Robyn, whom I hadn't seen in about a decade. Sitting on the laundry machines talking about shit we did together when we were kids (except for the being molested part), I was worried because I only had a half a bag of dope left and no syringe, definitely not enough to last me through the next day—especially if I had to snort it. But it was either that or nothing because I had no money to go anywhere and get anything anyway. (Yes, I see the overuse of any.) Just a return ticket back to Woodstock in my back pocket. So here comes the morning and I am so hungover I can't see. I can't believe I even drank. I don't know what came over me, older junkies usually can't drink unless they are fully kicked from heroin. I guess I was just nervous to be around my first real sexual experience, I was also pretty nervous that I was going to be the focal point after Grandma's surprise entry. I hadn't seen, talked to, or cared about any of these people since I was old enough to smoke my first cigarette. Why the fuck did I agree to this?

My hair was dyed a deep vixen, and I was most likely wearing eyeliner and had my nails painted. I had acquired this really cool brown suede jacket that was a little too small for me, but it felt like it looked really good, and my pants actually fit over my ass for a change. I really cleaned up for this little shindig. The VFW hall was just down from the papermill that my grandfather worked at his entire fucking life, and across the street from the old Foodtown where my dad took me once when I was around eight or so to get beer that he had to hide from my grandmother in the fridge under a head of iceberg lettuce in the crisper. I'll never forget that shit. It was the one time he had me alone since he and my mom split up. I probably hadn't seen him in like five or six years, and he took me to get a six pack. He came back to the house, drank three or four of them, and passed out in Grandpa's chair. My grandmother came home and asked me if he had been drinking, but before he passed out he told me not to tell her that he had been drinking. It was one of the first real lies I had ever told.

Okay, back to the reunion.

Balloons were strung together in bunches and hitting the ceiling in every corner. Colorful birthday cloths covered the fold-out tables and hung down to the brown and white diamond tiled floor as the long luminous bulbs covered in dead bugs bounced light off them and into my eyes, causing me to lose balance. Ultra-sized bottles of RC Cola and ShopRite ginger ale sat behind a giant punch bowl foamed to the top with a cheap bucket of sherbet. Plastic bowls filled with chips and doodles lined the middle of all the tables, while a thick layer of cigarette smoke darkened the air in the room. This may as well have been a "let's get cancer" party. I grabbed a red plastic cup and dunked it into the bowl hoping that maybe some pure cane sugar would make me feel a little better, but I was fucking dying, but I was young, so I could take it and still pretend to have the flu.

I was resting the side of my face on the table when I heard everyone muttering toward the door. Grandma must be here,

I figured. They turned all the lights off and brought her in for the surprise, and after almost giving her a mild heart attack, Aunt Marie slowly walked her over to me. I hadn't seen her in so long that she didn't believe it was me. She was older, grayer, shakier—it was fucking weird man. When you haven't seen the people who raised you in a long time, seeing them old is a trip. It's like finding out your favorite superhero is just some douchebag actor. Finally, after a while of convincing her it was me, she grabbed my hand and walked me around showing me off to everyone—all the aunts, uncles, cousins old and new. There were over 150 people there and most of them were severely overweight and chain smoking. All the cousins that I used to play with or look up to when I was younger were fucking massive now. I started to get anxiety and went back to my table in the corner to lay my head back down because I was starting to get weak, and that's when he walked through the door.

My "father," Joe.

My heart skipped a few beats when I heard his loud, obnoxious, very similar-toned voice. I looked up hoping he would notice me and come give me a hug. "For once in my life just please come be my dad and give me a fucking hug," is all I was thinking, but no such luck. He was surrounded by his brothers and sisters at the entrance of the door, hugging everyone and kissing everyone and laughing with everyone like he was the mayor of Rappise town. I don't know why, but I got up and walked over and waited behind everyone for a minute, but he didn't see me and I couldn't stand for very long, so I went and sat back down. The hope that he would notice me like I was the only person in the room was dead in the water. I gave up and eventually he graced me with his presence.

The last time I saw Joe I was sixteen. He came back to town, got remarried, and had another kid. We tried to make it work, but it wasn't in the cards. I was hoping with all my heart that maybe this time it would be different, though, when he brought me outside to talk. At last I was going to get some closure and hear some shit I'd been waiting to hear since I was a kid. Instead, he pulled out two unfiltered Camel cigarettes, put them both in his mouth, lit them, handed me one, and then proceeded to tell me that he had all this stuff he wanted to say to me, but it had all gone out the window as soon as he saw me. I was sick, cold, uncomfortable, and I just wanted this resentment to be done with, so I hugged him in forgiveness anyway and we finished our cigarettes and went back inside. That was it. The shit I'd been waiting to hear was nothing but a cigarette and a couple of shivering jokes. At the time I thought I had forgiven him, but I wasn't even close. I didn't even want to see this dude; I only came because my aunt guilted me into seeing my grandmother.

I had only seen my sister through glass at the hospital when she was first born. She wasn't there, but she had written me a letter and given it to Joe. When we went back inside he came over and handed it to me, and it started something like this, "I don't know you, but I love you." I read that and out of nowhere these feelings all started coming out of my eyes. I lost it. Junkies are hypersensitive as is, but add a little dope sickness to it and watch out, brother! The tears hitting that tile floor were almost as dangerous as the black ice in the driveway out front! I cried like I had never cried before, so much so I had to walk back out into the freezing cold and smoke another cigarette.

The plan was to go back to Aunt Marie's and take the bus to Woodstock in the morning, but instead I got so fucking emotional from reading that letter that when Joe offered to bring me back to his house and meet the family, I said yes. I didn't want to see him at the reunion, let alone spend a weekend at his house in wherever-the-fuck New Jersey, but I was so fucking out of my mind I have no idea what I was thinking.

The drive was a blur. Actually, most of this shit I am writing is a blur. About halfway there, Joe asked me if I was sober, like in AA sober. When he did that my face got a little hot and prickly, which meant I was about to lie to avoid some weird sobriety lecture. I told him I had almost thirty days clean, and then he told me how proud of me he was and how happy that made him. Then he started to tell me that he went to AA for years but didn't anymore because his family and God kept him sober. I got mad on the inside because it's like "fuck you dude, what gives you the audacity to think I would be even remotely interested in how you feel about what I do?"

When I was sixteen, I went into the Army recruiting office Joe worked at because it was right by my school. I wanted to surprise him, but I was in some weird phase in tenth grade, so my nails were painted and I was probably wearing eyeliner. I could see the embarrassment on his face when I walked into the building and the other boatheads he was in the room with started snickering. He rushed me into the back room and asked me why I was wearing all this girly shit. That was the last time I saw him I think. It hurt a lot, and apparently it still does. The point is that I couldn't believe I was in a fucking car with this dude that didn't pull out of my mother in time, and the sad thing is that I am only now realizing how much like him I actually am. It's absolutely terrifying.

My sister couldn't come to the birthday party because she was performing in a play at her school, which was where Joe ended up taking me. I sat in the back of this dark auditorium staring blankly at a stage full of children yelling some annoying song and smelling something in the air that can only be described as a bologna-flavored crayon and pizza day. And then this little girl with long blonde curls came up on my right side and said hi. I got up and gave her a hug and we all started crying, it was a very emotional moment. We went back to their house and watched some Chuck

Norris–type movie, then she took me up to her room with an old acoustic I found in the house and we wrote a song and used the letter she had written for the lyrics. By all circumstances this was a pretty decent day in the family repair department, and I was feeling pretty excited about everything.

The next morning when I woke up everything was bright and smelled super clean, which meant I wasn't dope sick anymore! I got up and stretched the last of the soreness out of my arms and legs and went to the bathroom. I was wearing boxer shorts and when I came out of the bathroom Joe was waiting in the hall. He saw I was only in my underwear and started sternly pointing his finger and telling me that is not how you walk around in his house and told me to "put some damn clothes on, what the hell are you thinking..." I was immediately infuriated. Who the fuck does this guy think he is yelling at me like he's my father? Fuck this asshole, I'm out.

I got on a bus back to Woodstock ASAP. And that was the last time I saw that dude.

JOHN THE BAKER

I FIRST MET JOHN in 1994 around the beginning of Beast through mutual friends. He worked in a bakery right off the main strip in New Paltz, a college party town about forty-five minutes south of Woodstock. If we were going down to get drunk and pickup girls, we would always try to get there before the bakery closed and John would hook us up with free pastry. John was an anarchy-charged, crust punk type of guy who would show up on the green in the height of tourist season and relentlessly hammer his acoustic guitar while screaming into the sky about things like corrupt cops, his girlfriend Jenny, the shitty local radio station, and how pathetic tourists and commerce were. He was also a part of the Eppard family, which is legendary in the Woodstock area. His nephews, Josh and Joe, had a band called Three that performed around town at the same time we were starting to get our thing together, and their father also had legend status playing blues at the local open mics. Joe and his dad never played with a pick, which used to blow my fucking mind.

It was really fun to get drunk and watch him terrify people in broad daylight from our little drinking spot across the green. I actually thought he was really psychotic until I talked to him and he turned out to be one of the most mellow, sweetest dudes on earth. The next obvious thing that needed to happen was that a band needed to be formed around this maniac. I immediately envisioned George and I pounding him in the ass from behind on the stage while he spit lyrics like loads of cum into a crowd of shitty Woodstock punks that would slather it all over their sweaty naked chests like it was the cure for the vaguely misguided anger in their completely wasted lives. I confronted him about it one day and he immediately said yes, and before we all knew it we were rehearsing in our buddy Solomon's barn, which oddly enough was the place that Beast recorded their second demo.

It was me, George, John on acoustic and vocals, and John's eccentric freakazoid buddy Dan on lead guitar. This fucking kid annoyed the shit out of me so hard and was normally someone I would never play with, but the flanged funk riffs that distorted out of his guitar brought something to the band that was undeniable and completely changed everything, making this thing some sort of freestyle funk punk jam that would last for hours.

Slimy Penis Breath was unfortunately finished as soon as it started for me because shortly after we got together, Jen and I took off for LA. So it was really cool for George and I to be able to come back and have it feel like we never left. I've always really needed music in my life; it has always been the one thing either saving or destroying me.

——

JOHN DIDN'T DRINK OR do drugs, just smoked weed and rolled hippy welfare cigarettes out of a can. He was older than the rest of us by a few years and inevitably took on the worried father roll since he had basically just adopted three junky sons. He was very empathetic to our dark and tortured souls.

We showed up high as fuck and usually late to every gig; we played in dresses and wore eyeliner. Sometimes we would play naked, and I usually needed a bucket behind my amp in case I threw up. It was one of the funnest bands I had ever been in. We didn't have a fucking care in the world except where the next high or show was coming from, and they always came. It was nice to finally forget about Los Angeles for a little while.

We made a live album from a show at the Rhinecliff Hotel. The cover of that record is a pig's head in a cop hat with a giant, veiny, cock for a tongue. The music was very reminiscent of the album cover...it was gross, dirty, honest, and raw as fuck. We had songs with names like "Crack Baby," "Fist Fuck the Pope," "Woodstock Punks Are Full of Shit," "The Cops Are Fucking Little Girls" (they were), and we played every show like it would be our last—because at that moment in time it could very easily have been.

Funny story about that last show. Funny now, anyway.

I showed up ten minutes before the gig was supposed to start to a nervous but relieved John waiting out front. I had taken a trip to the city and stocked up for the week with three bundles of Knockout safely tucked into the inside pocket of my puffy winter jacket and had barely made it back in time for the show. The pocket had a zipper so I knew that the drugs would be fine as I rolled it up into a ball and stuffed it under a bench next to the stage. Dan approached me right before we went on in his true annoying fashion and asked me for a bump, but I couldn't stand him and I didn't feel like bending back underneath that bench and getting it out, so I refused with pleasure. John was fighting with his girlfriend, George was fighting with Dan about something, and now Dan was mad at me too, but who gave a fuck. I was just pissed off in general because my life was so awesome. It turned out to be the best show we ever played, so good in fact that right after we vowed to always get into a fight before each show because it was that great.

All I wanted to do after the show was grab my jacket and go back to Woodstock. I had finally gotten out of K's and rented a room in a friend's house and was very excited to go sit alone in it and shoot dope all night. But here comes Dan again, whining about could he please please please have a bump, pretty please, Jason. I wanted to punch him in the face so badly, but instead I had enough to spare a tiny bump, and since he played such a great show and was probably my ride home, I took pity on him. I needed a bump anyway. I was a fucking wreck and had sweat out my soul during that show, along with all the dope, so I reached under the bench and grabbed my jacket, immediately noticing it was wet.

What I didn't realize before the show was that I had put my jacket directly under a leaky pipe. I frantically unzipped the inside pocket to save what I could, but it was already too late. The pocket was filled with water and the dope was gone. The bundles were all still held together with rubber bands, but all the dope had dissolved into the fabric of my jacket. I had no money to replace what I lost and couldn't get any dope for the next couple of days even if I did. When I got home I tried to ring out the sleeves into a spoon and shoot it, but it was useless.

The band played a couple of more shows but eventually had to go on without me, for I was a little too busy trying to rip my life apart and put it back together at the same time.

THE ROCKLAND FILES

HERE I WAS, SICK AGAIN and not knowing where the next shot was coming from. Keeping this lie going was so fucking exhausting that I didn't care who knew what I was up to anymore, I just wanted to never be dope sick again. What I believed to be the problem in hindsight was the cocaine. We started putting cocaine in the spoon along with the heroin, and anytime that happens you literally have about a month if you're lucky before your life goes further into the toilet than it already was. It's an impossible high to keep going even for someone with an endless supply of money. The high is just too fucking good.

I knew I couldn't keep this up for another day, so I did what any independent junky would do in a tough situation: I called my mommy.

Mom was still in Rockland county but was now separated from Ricky and had a new doctor boyfriend named David, who was apparently living at the house now and answered the phone when I made my distress call. I told him that something was terribly wrong and that I needed to come home, so he agreed to meet me at the bus station and we would deal with whatever it was when my mom got home from work. I was finally going to fess up and tell her everything, kick heroin, and get the fuck on with my shitty life. The look on this poor no-idea-what-he-was-getting-himself-into-when-he-started-dating-my-mother fucker's face was priceless when I told him I was a heroin addict. The burden that he was going to have to take on once my mother got home and found out about this was plastered all over his face. My mother reacts to emotions very poorly, like I do; it's where I get it from, obviously.

And from my experiences in dating mothers, I can tell you that the last thing a new boyfriend wants to do is get involved with the girlfriend's twenty-six-year-old man baby son's drug problems, especially one as extra man baby as I.

I got to the house and rested on my sister's bed. I must have passed out right away from exhaustion because the next thing I knew my mother was coming down the hallway with David. The closer she got to the room, the more my face got all hot and prickly. The look of confusion on her face when she walked into the room let me know right away that I had to just rip off the Band-Aid, so I blurted out that I was a heroin addict. And there it was, that look of disappointment I had been seeing on her face since I was in first grade. She immediately started ripping all of my sixteen-year-old sister Aimee's grunge posters down off the wall, screaming that it was all Courtney Love and Marylin Manson's fault, turning the rest of the day into an after school special. My poor sister came home to ripped posters all over her floor and a junky in her bed. The good news about all that is, I scared her so much she ended up never touching the stuff.

In proper Italian fashion, my ninety-seven-year-old great grandmother was spending the end of her days upstairs in the house with an older and very Irish Catholic nurse watching her during the week. Nani has been my guardian angel ever since she passed in '97, but before that she was my biggest fan. Unfortunately, I was too fucked up to spend her final moments on this earth with her, even though we were in the same house.

I woke up on the downstairs couch the next morning sick and alone. I could hear the television going in the upstairs living room, so I knew that the nurse was there with my grandmother, but everyone else was at school and work. I did my best to hide out as long as I could but eventually had to crawl upstairs to introduce myself because I needed to look in all the medicine cabinets for anything that would take the edge off. I immediately found some sleeping pills in my grandmother's bathroom and downed most of the bottle, but all that did was make me groggy. I was still dope sick, still in a state of the most uncomfortable annoyingness, but now I could also add lethargic to the list. The only thing that was making any sense in my brain was to get in touch with K and see if someone could come get me, but I just couldn't bring myself to do that, not after blowing up my spot and completely terrorizing my family. I needed to stay here and ride this out, maybe go back to school and learn a trade or some shit.

This bullshit had to stop. But also, there had to be something in this house somewhere to just make me feel a little better. I looked again in my mother's bathroom and found a bottle that said, "Take one pill daily for a slowed heart rate."

Well fuck me runnin'. I thought, if one pill slows down your heart rate imagine what five would do? Junky science always makes the best sense in the heat of the situation. I took five pills and went back downstairs to the living room hoping to feel better very soon.

My mother came home and walked past me completely ill-humored, not saying a word. She went upstairs and slammed her bedroom door loud enough for the people in Poland to hear it. The nurse left, and my sister came home from high school a little later and went into her room. Before I knew it the house was dark and quiet and everyone was asleep except me. I laid there feeling very offbeat. Something was happening under my skin, and I could

48

already tell that it was not going to end well, and I'm not talking about the bar that was digging into the middle of my back from the pullout couch. About three or four hours after I had swallowed the heart pills my arm started involuntarily bending backward, immediately followed by my leg and jaw. My bottom jaw was moving to the left and I couldn't stop it! I thought for sure it would snap in half. Snakes slowly constricted around the tree branches as I rolled myself up the stairs to my mother's bedroom and woke her up. She jumped up in a panic and raced me to Nyack hospital, but as soon as we pulled up in front of the emergency room my symptoms quickly and oddly subsided. All of the sudden I was fine. This poor woman begrudgingly drove back home and didn't say a word. We got back to the house and as soon as I laid back down it started up again, but this time the pain had doubled. I couldn't wake her up again, she would have fucking killed me. I had to just lay there and take it, hoping it would eventually stop. I thought my bones were going to pop through my skin. I have had many super shitty experiences in my life, and this was the absolute worst to date.

To make this situation even worse, I was watching Nickelodeon because old sitcoms from the seventies make me feel safe, but by now it was almost daylight so that fucking creepy kids show *Blue's Clues* was on, and I was too paralyzed to look for the remote. I just squirmed back and forth looking for some sort of ease while this weird dude in a striped shirt sang and danced with a big blue dog. All I could do was wish I was him, because he wasn't feeling any of this pain.

Daylight finally broke, which meant that everyone was going to start getting ready for work and school. I laid still like a possum until the house was empty and then I crawled to my sister's bed and hoped that this excruciating pain would just magically stop.

My bottom jaw was pushing against the left side of my face like it was trying to break itself off and my chest was so tight I couldn't get a deep enough breath for a yawn. A bag of dope would cure all of this immediately, so I finally broke down and called K. I couldn't talk because my jaw was locked to one side of my face, but she told me that George and the new guy Jimmy were making a run in the next hour or so. I somehow managed to mumble where I was and convinced her to send them my way. I didn't want to go back with them; I really did want to get better. I just didn't want to feel this way anymore, so I gave them my mother's address and told them to come and fix me on their way back up. As much agony as I was in, I still felt a little sigh of relief just knowing they were coming. I only hoped it would happen before anyone got home. Shortly after I hung up with K, my mother called. I tried to pretend I was sleeping, but the nurse kept yelling down to me until I finally gave in and picked up the receiver with my warped-ass hand. I dropped the phone on the bed and tried to lay my head next to the receiver so I could mumble that I was okay and then see how quickly it would escalate from there, but she hung up on me before any of that happened. I was somehow in the clear, all I had to do was wait a few hours before I was rescued by the junkies.

Ten minutes later an ambulance and two fire trucks screeched into the driveway. They rushed up the front steps past the nurse, throwing me onto a gurney and carrying me back out the front door. All the neighbors were peeking through their curtains and standing on their porches getting the show of the week as the unfriendly, quiet neighbor's junky son got tossed into the back of the ambulance! One of the many advantages of living in a cul-de-sac. They rushed me to Nyack hospital and threw me on a bed in the ER. The pain was so much worse now that they had been shaking me around, and it all happened so goddamned fast. I had to call K and tell her what just happened before they left for the city. I had to tell them to come to Nyack hospital instead of my mom's house. There was a phone on the wall and I crawled to it, lying there against the floor and the wall, trying to flip the receiver off the hook by the long curly cord hanging down. I couldn't stand up, so my only chance was to fling it off the receiver and onto the floor. Thankfully, the buttons were on the talky part of the phone. I miraculously got the phone off the hook and got a hold of her, but George and Jimmy had already left. My only hope was that they would call her when they got to the city and she could redirect. I gave her the number that was on the phone, and that was that.

Two nurses came in, one picked the phone up off the floor and hung it up, then both picked me up off the floor and put me into the wheelchair in the corner. They didn't even ask why I was on the floor, they just wheeled me down the hall talking to each other like I wasn't there. It didn't matter anyway. I never saw George or Jimmy that day.

I was placed in the maternity ward until a bed opened up in the detox, where I was supposed to be. This had a real potential to flare up one of my favorite fetishes. Wait, no, I didn't know I had that fetish yet.

Sorry.

I laid in a plastic bed, squirming and squealing, for what felt like five hours until a doctor finally walked into the room. He had a team of young students with him, and they were all holding clipboards. They circled the bed, staring down at me. I could open my eyes only enough to see the looks of confusion on most of their faces. I tried to ask the doctor what was happening to me but my jaw and neck were so sideways into the bed that I couldn't even make sounds anymore. I was just slurping while my arms twisted around uncontrollably.

The doctor explained to the group of hot, young, pleasant-scented students that this was the result of an overdose of Haldol. He then shot me up right away with eight hundred milligrams of Benadryl. I was fine almost immediately. I was sweaty, out of breath, and my entire torso was sore, but I wasn't dope sick at all and I finally finished that yawn, which felt good.

That was my first experience at the Nyack Recovery Center, and it sure as fuck wasn't my last. I would frequent that place and all the others like Norm from *Cheers* over the next whatever time frame this turns out to be...

CODY AND THE PRICE

I HAD DECIDED THAT it was the places I was living that were the problem. It was Woodstock, Rockland County, Los Angeles, rehab. All of these places were for sure causing the drama in my life.

My buddy Ben moved down to his mom's on the Upper West Side but would come back upstate on the weekends. Every Friday in the midafternoon I would sit on the green where the flag was posted and wait for Ben to come through town. He would pick me up and take me down the road to his dad's house, where we would spend most of the time shooting speedballs (cocaine and heroin mixed) in the upstairs bedroom. Every time he left I would spend the entire time he was gone wondering when he was coming back with more of that shit. He always had the best drugs and would fondly talk about his dealer Cody down in Harlem, so I would like to say that Ben was the one who prompted my move to NYC.

My grandmother lived on the Upper East Side right across the park from Ben's mom, so it made perfect sense that I make this more than a weekend party and convinced her to let me stay there. I moved onto the pull-out couch in her one-bedroom apartment and my plan was to get a job waitering at some swank sushi spot, maybe frequent some open mic nights until I got discovered, and have the record label move me back out to Los Angeles. I honestly had no idea how incapable of employment I actually was at this time in my life.

Ben worked at one of those fancy coffeehouses that made bread in the back. Every morning I would wake up sick and hobble across the park to sit out front of the place until he got off. When he finally did, we would jump into the back of a gypsy cab and head up to Harlem to meet Cody around 123rd and Broadway. From there he would walk us over to this little shooting gallery room on the first floor of this ratty old building. It wasn't too safe to be us and be in that neighborhood back then, so the quicker we got inside the better. Ben would hand Cody all the money he stole from work that day and off he would go, leaving us in this tiny room with nothing to sit on but an old futon mattress that was folded over and covered in what was most likely blood, vomit, and cum. I was always so afraid of what was actually in the fold of that thing. If early-eighties AIDS was a location, it would be this room.

A tiny sink hung on the center of the wall surrounded by handprints and blood swipes. There were probably some hard boogers stuck somewhere on there. Empty fast-food wrappers littered every corner, ripped up empty dope baggies and caps to syringes and crack vials were scattered everywhere along with some weird garments of clothing that were also stained with God knows fucking what.

This is definitely how a plague would begin.

The smell of the room was moist and pungent. It really seeped into your clothes and skin, but it was safer than being a white boy on any block in that neighborhood back then. Now that place is infiltrated with Instagram models who walk little dogs attached to Prada leashes.

We would get so antsy waiting for Cody to come back that we would tie belts around our biceps and just sit there waiting and pumping our hands to get the veins big and juicy. Every time the front door to the building opened and someone would walk down the hall, our hearts and breath would go silent as we sat motionless hoping it was Dr. Cody. But it was never him. He always took so fucking long to get back that when he did finally arrive our veins would be burst open with joy. He would push through the door that was only held shut by a balled-up rag tucked into the door hole mumbling the same thing every time, "The doctor is in, boys. The doctorrrrrr issssss innnnnnnn."

The doctor would never let us shoot up on our own. He always did it for us and honestly I didn't mind at all. He always hit the mark on the first shot. We would hold out our arms with the end of the belt tightly fastened in our teeth, panting like two starving chihuahuas waiting for dinner to be put in a bowl. His cold hard hands would grab my elbow and twist it toward him as he pulled the syringe from his lips and brought it down to the pit of my arm. I would see spots in slow motion and could literally feel the rush happening before the cold steel touched my skin. It was always so cold going into the building, but every time we left sweat would be pouring out of us as we skipped to the train station.

This became an everyday event, and after a successful day of scoring I would go back to my grandmother's, eat a pint of Häagen-Dazs while watching *The Matrix* on VHS over and over because it was the only tape I owned. The closest I came to trying to find employment was hitting a street corner on the Upper East Side with my acoustic and playing with the case open for about fifteen minutes before getting completely embarrassed and closing up shop.

I needed money, my habit was growing, and Ben couldn't carry the both of us forever. I remember passing a bunch of little stores near my grandmother's apartment with huge neon signs in the window that said, "WE BUY GOLD." I started sifting through my grandmother's jewelry when she was at work, picking out some things I didn't think she would notice missing. I went to the pawn shop with Ben and we got like a hundred bucks for a few little necklaces or whatever. Not a bad day for not doing any work, and that kept us high for like two days. I took a little bit more every day. I found the key to a locked cabinet in the living room and found the sterling silver. I also found the jar that Grandma kept her rent money in. I was completely out of control and knew what I was doing was horrible, but the sick part of addiction doesn't feel guilt for relatives—only the relief part does.

Within a little over a week I had taken everything. I took all the necklaces, the silver in the cabinet, Pop Pop's pinky rings, everything. I was about nine grand into hock by now and this last trip would score me around a thousand, making it an almost even ten that I had robbed from my poor grandmother. Ben and I went back to his mom's tiny little apartment, but after we got high, I didn't really know what to do. I couldn't go back to my grandmother's. Once she got home, she was for sure going to notice that everything was gone, and that would be it for me and my family. I thought about maybe staging a break in and calling the police, but I was way too fucked up for anything like that, so after a few more speedballs and some serious thinking, I decided to take a bus back to LA.

GREYHOUND ONE

I RAN BACK TO my grandmother's while she was still at work, grabbed my bass (with no case), and filled a brown paper bag with a few shirts and some CDs. I got to the port authority and checked the schedule. There was a bus leaving within the hour, so it was meant to be. Ben, myself, and my old roommate from Woodstock who just randomly happened to show up at Ben's mom's to get high, stood out on Forty-Second Street pounding dirty water dogs and saying our goodbyes, and off I went back to La-La Land.

The bus was full, but I was still able to get a seat by a window. The guy sitting next to me was completely bummed out because within the first hour I had probably gotten up to go to the bathroom six or seven times. I couldn't stop shooting up. That's the problem with cocaine, once you start mixing with the heroin, it's game over pretty quickly no matter what your status in life is. That high is so intense that it destroys your life and usually kills you within months if not weeks. With some people I'm sure it's days. Gnarly shit, man. The last time I sat back down in my seat, the guy started to tell me about this better way of life he had found and how he had been clean in NA for a month or so, what are the fucking chances. Out of all the people on the bus, in the giant of New York City, I get this fucking parrot-mouthed asshole sitting right next to me.

I remember feeling bad for him that he couldn't have any of my drugs and then getting up immediately and going right back into the bathroom. He disappeared a few stops into that trip, thank God, finally giving me my own little row. I only had two syringes with me and both broke before we got to Ohio, so by the time we got to the tip of Texas I had already snorted all of the drugs and spent the last day and a half squirming in my seat.

It was a late cloudy morning when we pulled into the Cahuenga Station at Hollywood Boulevard. I stepped off the bus feeling better than I should have for some reason, I think the smoldering damp Los Angeles smog was breathing life into my tarred lungs. I had no money and didn't really think about what I was going to do once I got to LA, I just knew that it felt good to be there again, and even though it was cold and damp it was still way warmer than New York.

The attendant unloading the bags from underneath the bus took my paper bag and threw it toward the pile. It hit the pavement and broke open sliding everything across the parking lot. He just kinda looked at me as to say, "Sorry, dude" as he flung more bags onto the pile. A woman looked at me almost with tears in her eyes, as I strapped my bass over my shoulder and started to walk away leaving whatever shit I had brought with me right where it was. I had formed a plan to surprise Jen, who I hadn't seen or barely talked to since the end of the last book. I headed east down Hollywood Boulevard in the general direction of where she was now living. What was she going to do when she saw me? If I could even find her at all, that is. All I had to go on was what Jeff had told me high as fuck on a phone call months prior. So I knew that her new place was across the street from Jeff's old singer's basement apartment on Lyman Place somewhere, and I had been to his apartment once or twice before so I didn't think it would be that hard to find her. It started to drizzle as I got farther east, and by the time I got to her general area it was pouring, and with no protection for the only thing I loved and possessed, I had to find shelter fast before my bass got ruined. I came to a church a block away from her street on the corner of Rodney and Prospect. I ran under the covered doorway to take refuge until the rain subsided. I stood there shivering in my soaking wet clothes while cars drove past. I felt like a homeless bum, though actually I was a homeless bum, I just didn't know it at the time.

I walked to the corner of Lyman Place and stared down the street wondering how my life was about to end up. Would Jen hear me as I walked from one end of the block to the other yelling out her name? It was raining hard again, and I was drenched, but I didn't care. I had left the bass tucked in the corner of the church overhang so I could take the time to find her. I had to find her. I had nowhere else to go. I was way too embarrassed to go to the Viper Room. I would have rather slept on cardboard than ring that fucking doorbell and beg for anything.

I walked up and down the block a few times, yelling louder with each pass, but nothing. I would go back to the church to take cover for a bit then go back down the block yelling. I wasn't even sure if she still lived there, but I just had no choice but to keep trying. It was getting dark and I had been out there for hours. I was starting to get really worried about my current situation. I figured I would make one more pass and then go find a nice warm public bathroom to sleep in or something, maybe try again the next day. Right then I saw a curtain move so I stopped and yelled one last time, and there she was staring at me from her window. She opened her front door and stood on the porch completely baffled as to what was happening. I approached with caution. I didn't know if she hated me or what, and here I was asking for shit. Here I fucking was again and nothing had changed, man, fucking nothing! Except this time I had to lie about it. I couldn't just show up back there worse than when I left, for crying out loud. But how fucking obvious must I have been. It was so good to see her, smell her apartment. It smelled just like the other place, and like her place in Woodstock before that. It smelled like home. I'm not really sure exactly what happened or how long I was there, but I do remember lying about being clean. I was always lying about being clean. She fed me and played me some new stuff she had been working on. She also played me the song she wrote that had my pathetic voicemails on them, which was a tad embarrassing. I think she even let me crash there for a few nights, but I obviously couldn't stay long. I wish I could tell you more about this trip, but it was a short one, and in hindsight was meant for Jen and I to kind of smooth things over, which we did. But I quickly realized by the next day or so that I just couldn't handle it in Hollywood anymore and that it was time to go home and face the music...

GREYHOUND II:
TWO REAL

I SHOWED UP AT the Viper Room to beg for another bus ticket home. It felt like I was just there in that goddamned fucking chair, snotting into a handful of black fucking bar napkins. My cousin, again, with the soul of an angel, gave me like eighty or ninety bucks and sent me on my way.

I had nowhere to go when I got home, and it was winter. What the fuck did I just do to myself? The bus ticket was only like sixty-seven bucks or some shit, and since I wasn't really eating that year I decided to go down to Third and Bonnie Brae first to get a balloon. The bus wasn't leaving until eleven the next morning so I had time, and I really needed to be high to sleep in the Cahuenga Terminal. My problem was that I thought the heroin was my problem, so I could just always have that to blame my life on. If I fucked up sober then that meant I was a fucking loser, not just a junky. That kept me fucked up for a really long time.

I scored and was quickly walking to go shoot up in the most disgusting Jack in the Box bathroom in all of the land when I heard a female voice from the distance behind me say, "Hey, you! Did you just cop?" I stopped and turned around, which normally in that area you don't do, but I smelled something sweet in the air that, combined with the gentleness of the voice, put an immediate spell on me. Standing there was this extremely pretty, short, business class white girl with reddish brown hair and a fancy crème-colored pants suit. She was definitely not the type that was usually down on that particular corner. This had to be a mirage, but no, she was real as fuck.

She said she just got beat trying to score and it was her last twenty dollars until tomorrow, and if I could share mine with her she would be forever grateful. I told her I would break her off a piece of what I had if she gave me a ride back to Hollywood. I was going to have to walk all the way back because I only had the exact amount for the ticket left in my pocket. She agreed and brought me to her car, a white Lexus. I asked her what she did for a living, she definitely had money. Turned out she was the producer on a new show called Real TV but wasn't getting paid till tomorrow. She was hot, but I was sick and not giving a fuck about how she would react, so I asked her if I could shoot up in her car. She told me she had never watched anyone do that before, and I could see her getting turned on. What a fucking freak, just my type.

We started making small talk as we pulled out of the parking lot, and when I got to the taking the bus home in the morning part, she asked me if I would spend the rest of the money I had left on more drugs and she would reimburse me in the morning *and* drive me to the bus stop in time to get back to my sealed death sentence. How could I refuse such a generous offer from such a beautiful woman? So I turned around and went right back to my guy for two more balloons. I figured I would save the last twenty for some junk food later since she was paying me back.

Now, let me explain the heaviness of this situation.

This was literally like receiving an inheritance email from a Ugandan prince. This type of shit just doesn't happen, especially to me. I mean, anything really terrible could have happened here, and should have—this setup was straight out of some I-end-up-being-hung-from-chains-and-brutally-tortured type of movie. But I had nothing to lose, and nothing to look forward to, and for the first time in my life I didn't fear death or what was going to happen next. She was staying at a hotel right on the beach in Santa Monica that Richard Nixon used to stay at, and why she had to tell me that I will never know. I mean, sure, babe. I get it. You're a super big deal, what with a homeless junky in your car.

I was not stoked on going to Santa Monica and having to be in Hollywood by eleven the next morning. I don't even know why I gave a shit. I was going back to something so fucking scary I might as well have just stayed in LA and hoped either this girl's creepy fiancé would jump out of the closet and they both cut me into little pieces while I was still alive, or if that didn't happen maybe I could just do what George did and cruise Venice Beach garbage cans for a few years before I die of a heroin overdose in Lari, Shala, and Allison's car park.

We pulled onto Ocean Boulevard, stopping in front of the hotel. She punched some numbers into a call box and the massive iron gate in front of us slowly crept open toward the car. I really feel like the place was surrounded by a massive stone wall covered in ivy with a giant blue neon sign exhibiting the hotel's name, but I was also high and it was a long fucking time ago, so let's just call it that for now. Let's say that the actual hotel itself was also covered in ivy. We parked and went straight up to the room so she could get high and maybe I could smell her shoulder. I sure as fuck wasn't getting hard for this poor girl. I don't remember much of the place, the bed was next to a window that looked out to the beach, and there was an old timey porcelain tub in the middle of the bathroom.

She started smoking the heroin, an obvious novice move, and after wasting it all in a giant ball of thick smoke she asked me if I had any money left. I told her about the twenty I was saving in case we got hungry, but she asked me if it was okay if maybe we bought some crack with it instead. Man, this girl liked to party! All I really wanted to do was see her naked, and I hoped that she kept her promise in the morning, but what the hell I was down to keep this adventure rolling hard for a few more hours. She didn't want to drive, so she had the concierge call us a taxi and had it billed to the room. Fancy last night in town type shit.

We jumped into an old yellow taxi that smelled like onions and the brim of a homeless guy's hat. We didn't drive too far, just far enough to where I had no fucking idea where we were. She waited with the taxi while I went into the alley to meet a tall, slim gentleman who had a bunch of crack where his teeth should have been. I handed him the twenty for food and he spit a massive rock into my hand. I dried it off with my shirt and stuck it right into my mouth. I don't even know what I was thinking. I should have just had him spit it right into my mouth instead of getting my hands all wet.

I came out of the alley just in time to see the taxi speed off, her looking at me helplessly through the back window. I couldn't even yell for them to stop because the cop was still right up their ass. I just had to stand there and watch as they drove off into the night. I had no fucking clue what direction to start walking either because she was wearing a short dress and I was staring at her legs the whole ride over. I went back into the alley to ask the dealer guy which way all the nice hotels were but he was gone. The hotel might have been in Venice but I wasn't sure, so I just walked along the beach and looked for the blue neon sign on the building covered in ivy. How fucking hard could that be? Apparently harder than I thought, because I was back and forth up and down that fucking strip for hours looking for this goddamn hotel, asking everyone who wasn't trying to purposely avoid me where this place could be. No one had a clue, and I was now starting to question if that girl or this place ever even existed. What if this was all just some crazy dream and I never even came out to California?

The dream suddenly turned into a nightmare now that I was out of money with no bus ticket and about twelve hours from becoming homeless George digging through trash cans on Venice Beach. I had to pee really bad, so I turned a corner to relieve myself behind a building and there it was: the fucking blue neon sign.

I scaled the wall next to the closed gate landing on a soft patch of grass. I wiped the sweat from my forehead and started looking around to see what my next move would be. All the windows in this superstructure were dark except for one, the one all the way at the top. This was most definitely her room. She had to be the only crackhead that could afford to stay here, and I had no way of getting up there. It was at least four in the morning by now and I was so crazy from drugs, sweat, and tears that I didn't dare go to the front desk—not like I'd have known who to ask for anyway.

I found a drainpipe covered in long thick strands of ivy that went all the way up to the roof and right past that window with the light on. I grabbed onto the branches and started climbing. I made it all the way up to the window and holy fuck, there she was. I couldn't believe it. I was just a little too far out of reach, though, so I swung hard and hit the window with my hand before being flung around the corner of the building almost falling to my death, which at this point in my night would have been a more than welcomed accident. Luckily that first hit got her attention and she ran over and pulled me in.

I was stripped of my clothes and placed in the steaming bath that she had run for herself. The hot water kneading into my sore leg muscles was better than any sex, and it felt good to not be pacing up and down the beach in a homeless panic.

She held a lighter to the crack pipe hanging from my lips while sweeping away all the sweat and dirt with a coral loofa. I had gone from total panic to complete euphoria in a matter of minutes. And as fucked up as we were, we tried to have some sort of sex afterward, but all I really remember about it is lying there naked while she nonchalantly told me about her psycho boyfriend who was in prison, but hired a private investigator to follow her and how she thought he was outside in his car.

I woke up in the morning and she was gone. I had no idea what time it was, if she was kidnapped by the PI, if she was ever coming back. There was a phone on the nightstand next to the bed, which I used to call Ben and ask if he wouldn't mind picking me up with a loaded syringe in a few days. I had no idea when or if I was going to get back there, but I needed to make sure that I had something set up just in case.

Finally, after about thirty minutes of distress, I heard her come through the front door. She came into the bedroom out of breath and told me not to make any noise. I heard a man's voice through the wall. I thought this was it, that I was fucking dead. I couldn't go anywhere unless I wanted to scale back down the drainpipe, so I just sat there in the bed hoping it would be painless and quick.

Where I grew up in New Jersey there is an old urban legend circulating about how this guy let a girl he just met tie him up to a bed in four-point restraints in a New York City hotel room. Then a giant black man in a Batman costume kicked in the door and raped him and he had to get a lot of stitches in his butt. That was all I could think about until she came back into the bedroom and threw a bunch of twenties at me.

It was now almost ten and we had to get moving if we were going to cop one last time and make that bus! I couldn't believe she'd actually came through and that I still didn't know her fucking name!

We went and copped a few balloons, but I couldn't get any syringes because it was too early, and the one I had was pretty messed up. I hoped it would last the trip. I was looking behind us the whole way to see if we were being followed, and when we got to the bus stop and she got out to give me a hug goodbye, I swear I saw him take a picture of us from the corner of the lot. I never got butt raped by Batman or jumped from behind by a strange ex-cop in a Hawaiian shirt. I also never got her name.

SAINT MARIE

I CALLED BEN COLLECT from every payphone at every stop we made from Vegas to Newark just to make sure he knew what day and time I was getting there. The shitty needle that I brought with me broke before the bus even got to Nevada, so I was forced to stick little pieces of tar up my nose and pinch it closed until they dissolved, then tilt my head back while it slowly dripped into my nasal cavity, hopefully getting me more high than sick to my stomach. It didn't work in the first book, and it sure as fuck wasn't working now.

I started to get sick somewhere in Oklahoma, and by the time we got to the southern tip of Pennsylvania my mind had tricked me into believing I was going to die if I didn't stick a needle in my arm in the next twelve hours. Ben agreed to meet me with the loaded rig when I got there, and once again, before I knew what hit me, I was sitting in a stall on a piss covered toilet that was full of shit and God knows what else in one of the gnarliest bathrooms in the world. But fuck, it felt so good to finally stick the needle in my arm and push all that garbage into my veins. I rode that lit fuse all the way down to the powder, but my reality had gotten way too intense for drugs to make it go away. I was combining two of the hardest drugs you could do, shooting them straight into my bloodstream, and it still wasn't enough to make the worry disappear.

That's how much of a fuck up I am.

Now that I was home, I had to figure out where the fuck I was going to go. I spent the night at Ben's mom's and took the bus up to Woodstock the next morning. I stepped off the bus and onto the green not having anywhere to go and definitely not feeling safe, so I ran down to see my friend Tony, who lived in a little bachelor pad down behind the anus (what we called the little parking lot in town) and begged him to let me live on a pile of his dirty clothes in the corner of his tiny one room apartment. All I had to do was feed him dope every now and then for rent and climb in and out through the window and I was good. My mom had blown up my spot with Scott and Kelly, who I'm pretty sure were still pissed about the wedding and had been driving around town looking to kick my ass and take me to rehab, so being outdoors was not in my best interest.

Being a heroin addict is the last thing you ever want to become. I needed a fucking break, but I couldn't go to my mom or anyone on that side of my family, so I called my father's sister, Aunt Marie. My cousin Bobby (Robyn's brother) was a heroin addict when he was younger, so I called in a Hail Mary to see if she would help me, and thank fucking Moses she said yes. I didn't know what else to do, so back the fuck down I went on that goddamned bus.

This book should be called the "Bus-ketball Diaries..."

So here I am at Aunt Marie's again, but this time there's no birthday party, no booze in the basement, no giggling cousins molesting me. Just me alone and dope sick and sitting on a small leather couch in the den while static from a police scanner nearby spikes my anxiety levels. I wrapped myself in a small, itchy quilt, and bawled my eyes out watching MTV News. The singer from

Sublime had passed away from an overdose, and Scott Weiland had just gotten arrested coming out of a dope house somewhere in NYC. If there was ever a sign to stop doing dope this should have been it, but all it did was make my joneses worse. My aunt came into the room and I told her that the guys on TV were my friends. I didn't know either of them. I was just embarrassed because I was crying. I did meet Scott at the Viper Room once and asked him if he wanted to do dope with me, but he replied, "My wife probably wouldn't like that very much and she's sitting right over there." That was the extent of our relationship.

Uncle Bob was dead, and Bobby and Robyn had moved out, so it was just Aunt Marie and me in this big house. I was excited to be there and really wanted to be done with all this bullshit and it felt like my last chance. It also felt really good to be back in Jersey after all this time. It still smelled exactly the same, and all the restaurants that I loved growing up were still there. Nothing had changed at all.

Aunt Marie had no clue what to do with me, and without me knowing, she called Joe to come over because he was an alcoholic who got sober, relapsed, and got sober again. He had knowledge of all this alcoholism stuff and could help her out a little, I guess. It was the least he could do considering that this was the only thing he ever gave me besides a receding hairline. Thanks, Dad.

I wasn't super excited to see him, but I came out of the den anyway and sat in the dining room on one of those Viking chairs with my head on the table until they eventually decided that I should go to a detox. It was a Friday, and the only reason I remember going to detox on a Friday was because just like every other county-funded hospital, Newark University's doctors take off for the weekend, leaving you helpless and sick with a good for nothing nurse by your side to do absolutely nothing but throw you shade for a few days. Also, at the time, Newark was the murder capital of the United States, and the detox was on the same floor as the AIDS ward. Remember AIDS in the nineties? It was like a George Romero film up in that motherfucker.

I was literally the only white guy in a sea of gay Black men crusted in puss filled sores and pacing back and forth past my room with the backs of their bloodstained gowns breezing open so I could see the dried shit that had dripped onto the backs of their bony little legs. I laid in the fetal position, facing the window.

The next morning, I rolled over to let the angry nurse check my vitals and noticed that a few of the patients had gathered around the outside of my door. It felt just like the dorm at county jail, except I didn't have to sleep on my sneakers. When the nurse left, one of the patients came in and dropped a couple of little orange Xanax next to my pillow, the same little orange Xanax that I used to crush up and snort at K's when we didn't have any dope. Those sweet sick men definitely helped that weekend pass by quicker than it normally would have.

Monday came, and a doctor finally showed up to tell me that I couldn't have methadone or any of the other fun things junkies like to use to prolong not getting their shit together ever. This made it pointless for me to lay in that cold hard bed when I could just do the same thing at Aunt Marie's on a real mattress. I could also have those weird NA guys come pick me up for meetings and actually get this life shit moving.

There was this meeting in Garfield that my new friend Dave would take me to that had a piano I would lie under. The cold dirty floor felt so good on the side of my face, and it was the only relief I was getting at that point. Especially after listening to whiny toothless assholes bitch about nothing for an hour and a half. After the meeting I would go back to the attic that Robyn used to touch me in and stare at the ceiling all night until the sun came up. I don't think I slept for like three weeks. I gradually started eating a little, doing a few push-ups, smiling when someone said something funny. I felt like I was finally ready to make my mommy proud for once, and it felt like the blade was off my throat and I could finally breathe without hesitation or fear.

Everything was going great. I started going to meetings regularly and getting acquainted with all the old Italian guys that would share about using eye droppers and sewing needles to shoot up on rooftops in Brooklyn, which I thought was just fascinating, considering my syringes were always broken. There were a bunch of people my age, most of whom were covered in tattoos, chain smoking Marlboros, and living what seemed to be content lives without drugs. The girls were hot and horny, the guys were funny and helpful—it was a pretty cool time to get clean. I got a little job behind the deli counter at a ShopRite that I could walk to and was realizing very quickly that it was so much fucking easier living this way rather than the way I had been for the past few years. Aunt Marie totally had my back, Mom wasn't worrying, and shit felt like it was finally gonna be okay.

The NA dudes would take turns picking me up every night around six. They would bring me to a meeting, buy me a cheeseburger and a milkshake after, then drive me home. They never breathed brainwashy shit into my face ever, they just showed me what they called a "clean way of living," and I was super into it. They all became fast, dear friends that I very quickly realized my life depended on.

There was Dave, a young, cocky, good-looking kid full of piss and jade who I got on with like we had been friends since birth. Benny had a tarantula tattooed on his neck and would pick me up blasting Sepultura. Big Drew, the massively overweight mope, always lagged behind unless we were going to a diner, then he was always the first one out of the car and through the door. There was other Andrew, a crazy white Rasta who called me "Rogue" every time I would say my name in a meeting because he loved the "Rogue For Life" tattoo on my ankle, and so many more...

The cute girls with tattoos paid attention to me, the dudes made me feel like I was actually cool, and I couldn't have been happier to be alive. I got a week clean, then two weeks, then three! This shit was flying by and I was just about to get my thirty day chip. There hadn't been a day that I wasn't "mood stabilized" since I was eleven years old, so this was a huge deal. I was really digging the attention as well. At every meeting I would stand up and announce my day count; the closer I got to thirty, the louder people would clap and pat me on the back. I didn't think I had to get a sponsor or work any kind of program, I just thought that hanging out smoking cigarettes, flirting with girls, and listening to pretty interesting stories would keep me clean. I got wind that an old friend, John, who had been a coke dealer pretty much my entire life, had overdosed and died in K's bathroom, which solidified my deal in NA. I didn't want any part of that shitty life anymore and was glad to be far away from it.

In meetings they told me over and over again to stay away from all my old friends. I heard "people, places, and things" in every meeting, but I didn't really understand what it meant. When I would share about wanting to go hang out because I missed them, this one old dude would keep saying that if I kept going to the barber shop I would eventually get a haircut. I thought, what the fuck are you talking about, old man? That part of my life was the happiest of my entire youth! Any given night there would be from five to forty of us hiding behind some factory or in an abandoned lot next to a mercury stream pounding tiny little bottles of Budweiser and choking on Marlboro Reds with little to no care or consequence. Banging girls with big hair and stonewash jeans in the back seat of Billy Van's powder blue Buick in the rain behind the A&P. Pounding burgers down our throats on ninety-nine-cent whopper Tuesday in the Burger King parking lot off Route 17 and waking up late the next morning not knowing how you got home, with sesame seeds and ketchup dried to your face. What a beautiful time to be alive. How the fuck was going to see my old friends who'd never even touched heroin going to make me want to shoot it again? So what if they drank and did blow on the weekends? They were still my friends, and that shit was never my problem anyway.

All of a sudden this little man came into my head out of nowhere and started telling me that meetings were bullshit and I could totally drink with my old buddies, maybe even get a job driving a truck with Billy or Jerry and be a weekend warrior normie like them because being in Woodstock was the whole reason I was a junky anyway. All I had to do was just stay away from there and I'd be fine. I started to get thirsty and all I wanted to do from this point on was be a normal working guy and hang with the old homies again.

I went into work and looked at my boss who was close to my age, and had the largest, shittiest Punisher skull tattooed across his entire chest, and I was also positive that this job was his life's career. No fucking way was I about to make this dude my best friend and that place my life job. That day I was given a paycheck for something around the tune of $167.00 that I was able to cash in the store. It was also the first time I had money in my hand that I actually earned since the last deli. I was twenty. I couldn't control the urge to want to celebrate, so I walked over to the payphone and called my old friend/neighbor Gillen. I had him come pick me up at the supermarket right away because no time could be wasted, my taste buds were salivating for something destructive and painful.

After I hung up with him, I called Aunt Marie and told her that I was going out with a friend from NA and would probably stay over at their house that night. I wanted to be a normal dude more than anything, and I really felt like I could pull it off.

But tonight, tonight we gonna party like it's 1989.

Gillen had a Pathfinder very similar to K's, and when he came ripping into the parking lot of the ShopRite to pick me up I couldn't help but feel that dope chill run up the back of my neck when I saw it, it was like being pissed on by my favorite porn star all over again.

It had been a minute since I was in the old neighborhood. I hung my head out the window like a dog as we cruised down the boulevard I grew up on. Passing by the bus benches that I would catcall girls from as a drunk teenager while listening to Theatre of Pain or Among the Living on my double cassette deck boombox, passing by the park where we used to smoke Reds with Willie the overweight forty-year-old virgin whose face was bright red from alcoholism, wore the same flannel every day, and still lived with his mother.

It was so nice to be back. I couldn't wait to get fucking hammered.

The first place I wanted to go was JJ's, one of my favorite old watering holes. So we got a nice buzz off of a few Dr. Peppers (a shot of amaretto dropped into a mug of beer), got some blow from Gillen's stepdad, and went to a strip club that an old flame was working at. I walked in and threw every dollar I had at the first stripper I saw hoping she would fuck me. I almost fucking had her, too, when out of nowhere Jerry and Mike from Alice in Chains walked in fifteen minutes before closing and ruined everything. I remember getting legitimately mad at her like she was my girlfriend.

We ended up back at Mike's, where I passed out all angry on the couch watching the sun come up just like old times. Nothing terrible happened, no-one died, and I didn't do heroin. I knew those creepy fucks in NA just couldn't handle their shit. I was relieved to find out I was nothing like those losers…

The next afternoon I slowly made my way back to Aunt Marie's, she didn't notice anything unusual, even though I was so hungover I could barely see and probably smelled like the floor underneath a bar mat. A week had passed since I'd been to a meeting or went to work. I would write songs in the bedroom until it was time to get drunk and tell my aunt I was going to a meeting. I was having the best time. Reconnecting with the normal life was just what I needed.

I was planning on working it out so that I could become a regular old blue-collar schmuck just like the rest of them, but then out of nowhere, Paul called me.

OFFICER PAUL

PAUL WAS PART OF my circle of friends in NA. A nice older guy with a red cop moustache who always wore a light-blue Members Only jacket and a trucker hat to cover his bald spot. My aunt yelled up to me to come get the phone, and when I came down the stairs and picked it up I could tell immediately that something was wrong. His voice sounded shaky and he was nervous. He started to explain how he had heard that I wasn't in the program anymore, so I immediately cut him off to tell him how I was doing just fine and didn't need him calling to try and brainwash me back to his bullshit cult.

He then proceeded to tell me that he wasn't trying to talk me into coming back, but that he wanted to get high and was wondering if I could go to the city because he looked too much like a cop and no one would sell to him. "Absolutely not," I said with vigor. I wasn't a fucking lowlife junky anymore; how dare he think such an appalling thought? He begged me saying that he would drive, pay for it, and that he even had a fresh syringe we could use (Big Drew's diabetic mom always kept a syringe on the table in the kitchen and he apparently took it). I got off on letting him try for a few minutes before I politely hung up and went back upstairs. Sorry, you pathetic old loser that can't handle your addiction, but I'm fucking cured so you can go suck the dealer's dick.

I didn't even feel the switch happen in my brain. There was no "maybe this is a bad idea" or even an "I think I will turn around and call him back." I just kind of came to with the phone ringing against my ear and I was calling him back.

I told my aunt that I needed to go help a struggling friend in the program and that I didn't know when I would be back, which technically wasn't a lie. Paul pulled up in his gold Acura twenty minutes later and off to Spanish Harlem we went. We pulled up to the corner I had always pulled up to, it hadn't been that long since I was there, but it felt like years had gone by and now I was scared. I copped a few bags, ran back to the car, and headed back to his apartment in Clifton.

Paul lived alone on the second floor of a two-family house on a quiet but congested suburban block. It was dark and absolutely freezing outside with long patches of blackened snow alongside the cars parked bumper to bumper on the wet street. The stairs to his apartment were steep and the hallway was hot. The sweat beaded from the heat and the fact that I was about to ruin my life once again. I already knew I was in over my head and there was no going back to Aunt Marie's after this.

It was a typical one-bedroom Ikea-furnished apartment for a single guy, like Peter Gibbons in *Office Space*. I de-robed all of my winter gear in the kitchen, (a couple of T-shirts over a thermal that used to be white) and walked into the living room, tossing the baggies onto the coffee table. Paul entered from the kitchen with two fresh glasses of water, spoons, and the syringe. I went and got the bleach from the bathroom, because Paul was from the seventies when they used to just share needles without cleaning them.

He sits across from me in this Archie Bunker–type chair, watching intently as I split the first bag into both spoons. He told me it'd been almost ninety days since he'd done heroin. It had only been thirty or so for me, so I did the first small shot just to test how strong it was. Which I'm glad I did, because it was a pretty potent batch. It was so good that I ran straight to the bathroom and puked. I came back to the room dripping in more sweat and fixed up a very tiny shot for Paul. I only gave him half of what I did because I knew a regular shot would have killed his old ass before I was able to sit back down on the couch. That's how most people die from this shit. These idiots come into the program and stay clean for a few weeks or months and think they can go right back to the normal amount that they used to do, and boom—dead.

Paul nodded out on the couch hard, and at the same time vomit rushed up my windpipe bringing me right back into the bathroom. I must have been in there for a minute because when I came out he was about to stick the needle in his arm again. I tried to stop him, but my mouth filled up with puke and I had to run back to the toilet. By the time I got back he had already done the shot. I asked him if he was okay, and he responded quickly with a yes. I let out a little sigh of relief, but something wasn't right. His hands were placed calmly on his lap, but his legs were trembling and his mouth was the shape of a tiny powdered donut with white foam encompassing his lips. I slapped him across the face as hard as I could, which brought him out of the death chamber he seemed to be crawling into. I asked him again, "DUDE, ARE YOU OKAY!?" He looked at me a little slower this time and answered yes again. I wanted another sigh of relief to happen, but I knew I was fucked. Talk about someone blowing your fucking high, man.

I knew I was about to lose him, so I slapped him twice as hard as I did the first time—once with the left, then again with the right. It was hot in the apartment and my eyes were burning from all the sweat. I'd never had to save anyone from overdosing before. He convulsed himself from the chair to the floor, landing on his side, his eyes screaming at me to save him as he laid there frothing onto the shitty brown carpet. He was turning blue and looking directly through my soul. His face turned from pink to purple within seconds. This dude was about to die right in front of me. I had run out of ideas and I'm not a fucking scumbag, so I called 911. I cooked up one last shot, figuring I was probably going to jail soon, and started scurrying around the apartment looking for an address to give to the operator. All I knew was that I was in Clifton, I think. I found a piece of mail stuck to the side of the refrigerator with a banana magnet and ran back into the living room to get rid of all the dope and paraphernalia before the cops showed up. There was nothing I could do for him at this point, so I ran downstairs and hid everything under the tire of a car parked a few houses down the street. I heard the sirens screeching around the corner as I ran back up the stairs, immediately jamming the loaded rig into my arm. I pulled it out and shoved it into my underwear as the paramedics burst through the door and started CPR. I stood there watching, sweating. As the cops started to question me I could feel blood running down my arm and made a fist when it started dripping off of my ring finger hoping they wouldn't notice. Thank God I was wearing a long-sleeved shirt. I snapped into "get out of jail free" mode real quick and told them that I was a friend from NA that he had called because he wanted to get high. I came to talk him out of it but that was how I found him when I got there. They bought it and told me that it would probably be best if I left. I backed their decision hard and gave them my name and the number to my mom's house before I bounced down the stairs into the cold, dark suburban question of how the fuck I was getting out of there and where the fuck I was going.

I hit the sidewalk, grabbed my dope, and watched from the end of the block as they put Paul into the ambulance. I heard one of them yelling for Narcan, a drug that drains the dope from your system in a very rapid and shocking manner. I started walking as the ambulance drove by me whooping the siren. In hindsight I should have grabbed his keys and taken his car, it's not like he was gonna need it any time soon. Instead, I ended up trudging through the exhaust-covered snowbanks on Route 46 for the remainder of the dark morning. I walked past an old trade school that I had gotten thrown out of when I was a teenager and thought that maybe I should have paid more attention back then. The glitter of the night sky was fading fast and I had to figure something out. By then I kind of knew where I was going and just kept pushing through the slush and snow until finally ending up in my old neighborhood, at my buddy Jerry's apartment.

ONE MORE TIME

A FEW YEARS AFTER high school, my family moved up to Stony Point, NY, and I couldn't fathom the idea of leaving New Jersey and not being able to drink with my friends, so I moved in with my buddy Jerry and his family in Hasbrouck Heights. This lasted about a year or so before I moved back to Woodstock, and even though I hadn't seen him in quite some time, Jerry was the type of friend who no matter what, you could show up unannounced at six in the morning and he would let you in and give you a couch—which is exactly what happened.

Jerry was now living with his girlfriend in Carlstadt, down the street from where I grew up, and I luckily got there right as they were both leaving for work. They were normal people and didn't know anything about heroin, but Jerry had a disdain for addiction because his mother died from alcoholism. I didn't want him to judge me or throw me out, so to be safe I lied and told them the same story I told the cops. They also bought it and let me chill there while they went to work. I crashed hard on the couch as soon as they left and didn't really wake up until they got home.

The night before's lesson was hard learned, and it turned out that those toothless losers in NA were right after all. I was done doing dope and ready to go back to those shitty meetings, I just needed to hang out at Jerry's for a day or two and clear my head. So I went into the bathroom and flushed everything I had left down the toilet. When Jerry and his girlfriend got home from work, one of them went into the bathroom and found a bag of dope on the floor. I guess I was still high from the night before and didn't notice that one had fallen to the side. I tried to come clean, but it was too late and they told me to get the fuck out. I really meant what I said about not doing drugs anymore and getting my shit together, but I had also woken up that fucking gorilla lying dormant on my back. I convinced myself that I was too ashamed to go back to Aunt Marie's and instead of dealing with it like a man, I took a bus back upstate and went to see if that room I was renting was still available.

The entertainment factor in our risky adventures was extinct. The numbing mask of warmth and affection that heroin used to give me and my friends had now turned dark, weird, and somewhat evil. There was no more sharing, no more laughter, no more light at the end of the hopeless tunnel. Hustle, greed, and a longing to be normal was all it was. People were dying, overdosing, getting arrested, and it was becoming obvious that everything was coming to an end. But junkies will hold on to that last thread as long as they can, which is exactly what we were doing.

One day K, Richie, and Dan went down for a pickup, but it had been hours past the time that they were supposed to be back. I laid there sick wrapped in a comforter on this shitty futon mattress in my tiny little room, occasionally crawling out into the living room to call Anna, who was also sick and waiting across town like I was to see if they had called her. The water in the house of the room I was renting reeked of sulfur, and every time someone turned on a sink I wanted to kill myself. Finally, right after I pissed the bed around midnight, the phone rang. I anxiously made my way to the phone, and as the receiver touched my ear I heard a dog barking and a bunch of cop radios in the background, and after a long pause, K's shaky voice said my name. I knew right away that I wasn't getting any dope that night. She asked me if I could come get her dog at the police station before they took her to the pound, I angrily declined, and that was the last time I spoke to her.

The cops pulled them over in the Pathfinder at a stop sign on the corner of 375th and 212nd in Woodstock, literally a mile away from K's house. It wasn't out of the ordinary to get pulled over right there, but it was pretty unusual for the cops to roll up there in five or six cars with their guns drawn and yelling at everyone to get out of the car and down onto the ground. I heard they almost shot that fucking dog because it wouldn't stop barking.

The story that I heard was that Dan sold some young girl dope a week or so before and she almost died and ratted him out to her parents and he got arrested, so to get out of trouble Dan ratted out K and Richie. Junkies are just like mobsters: they'll rat anyone out to keep the freedom train running.

I was thinking to myself that there was no way in hell it could end like this, but I was way too fucking sick to do anything about it, so I just laid on the couch and cried. Right then the phone rang again, and it was Anna. She wasn't ready to let it go either, so we drove down to Spanish Harlem at midnight on a weekday. Driving out of town was so fucking nerve-wracking, we were the only car on the road and we didn't know if we were being watched or what. All we knew was that we needed to not be sick anymore. So we took the back roads out of town in Anna's white Jetta and flew down to the city, trying to come up with scenarios of what could have possibly happened on the way. We couldn't believe it was finally over. I held my breath and looked in all the mirrors for like an hour until we finally got far enough away that it was obvious we were not being followed.

I was able to cop a bundle very easily at three a.m. on a street I had never been to before, because no one was out at our regular spot and we were back home by five. We drove twenty miles extra past our exit and came up the back way in case the cops were waiting again on Route 212 in some sort of sting operation.

What I didn't realize was that the only good bag of dope in the bundle I got was the one the dude pulled off the top and let me test; I gave the other half of that one to Anna to get well for the drive home and didn't bother to check the rest until we got back to town. When I got back to my place I ripped open a bag and put it in the spoon, and it was then that I realized all the rest of the bags were baby powder. I ended up trying to shoot NyQuil gel caps until about seven, my arms swollen and bleeding everywhere, and I had exhausted myself to a complete state of worthlessness. I was done. I could feel how done I was in my aching arms. I didn't need a detox or a rehab, I just laid down right where I was and didn't get up until it was all out of my body.

ROGUES

WE SPENT MOST OF our youth tripping in the woods, smoking our parents' weed, and drinking from the Devil's Spring on the green. I still love all those rogues with all my heart, we will always be Rogues for Life. Most of us have this force of dark light tattooed on our ankles, but that is a chapter for the book I will write when these are finished.

K's bust had left most of us completely freaked out and no one wanted anything to do with heroin anymore. It's not every day you get to escape the fate that junky life has in store for you. It was crazy for my junky friends and I to be hanging out on the green like we were fifteen again, to have a new freedom ascend from the clouds and bless us like this, only to become the old guys at the high school keg party, intimidating the teens and drinking all their beer. Every town has them, those guys that are just old enough to buy the beer and kick your ass but who still live with their parents and don't really have a steady job and will also try to sleep with your seventeen-year-old girlfriend after pounding a few red plastic cups. The big thing for me was that all my old friends were just so happy that I was off heroin that no one was mad at me anymore for all the dumb shit that I pulled. Being able to roam freely without having to watch my back was invigorating

My old bff and I kicked off that summer on the green with a couple of lawn chairs and a sign that said, "NEED TO DRINK! PLEASE DONATE!" We made almost two hundred bucks that day and got everyone hammered that night. We were the most charming scumbags you never wanted to hang out with, but were always there anyway. We were rogues and damn proud of it.

George and Anna were pretty much the only ones still stuck in the dope game. We would see them slinking through town every now and again in Anna's Jetta and shake our heads in judgement because we were the lucky ones, literally the chosen few. We were just so fucking happy to not be dope-sick slaves anymore, and there was never even a tiny urge to go back to that life.

We partied our fucking asses off that summer. We would all walk down the hill to Cumberland Farms, tie our jeans at the bottom, and fill our pants with as much St. Ides Special Reserve as we could and walk right into the woods with it. No one that worked there ever said shit. We found out that the beer cooler had a delivery door that led to the outside and wasn't locked, so we would pull a car up, pop the trunk, sneak into the cooler, and fill the trunk. We did that for a good month or so before they caught on and started padlocking the door. One time I was so hammered and hungry that I stumbled in, loaded my pants with Hostess cupcakes and shitty uncooked microwave cheeseburgers, Snickers bars, etc. I walked up to the counter to buy a pack of twenty-five cent gum so the lady wouldn't suspect anything, and she just looked at me with her one good eye and said very calmly, "Put it all on the counter, junior…"

JUNIOR?! Who the fuck did she think she was referring to?

I was like a twenty-six-year-old man child! I locked in on her one good eye and mumbled, "Go fuck yourself" or something and walked out to the parking lot. A moment of clarity crept into my blurry thoughts and I unloaded everything right where I stood and booked it into the woods before the cops showed up.

The next day I went into town to mooch some food off of whichever friend was working behind whatever counter to ail my hangover, and the cops immediately rolled up when they saw me and asked me where I was the night before. I figured they got me on the security cameras, but I didn't even make it that hard, it turns out that when I dumped all the shit out of my pants I had a piece of mail in my back pocket that landed gently on the top of the pile of cheeseburgers and sugared treats to make it super easy for the cops to solve the whodunnit. I was written a ticket with a court date and sent on my way, but I did not show up for court and got arrested drunk walking down the highway a few weeks later and spent a few days in county, which was how we paid fines back then (this line was stolen from Jack Grisham).

This debauchery lasted for a few more months. I was so free, and so hammered. No one seemed to give a shit about anything we were doing, and there were rarely any consequences. It was like we were given a free pass by the town because we weren't all strung out and stealing shit or overdosing all over the place. And there were just enough of us middle-aged man babies acting this way to make it not seem completely sad and creepy.

Then one drunken night at Tinker Street Cafe, I decided that it would be a fantastic idea to shoot some heroin.

So much time had gone by. So many peaceful days and nights with not one urge to completely ram my soul into the ground, and then BLAM-O—out of fucking nowhere, I'm on a mission that doesn't end until it's in my arm. The number one killer of junkies is when they think they can just do it one more time.

I stumbled down the street to a house where I knew people were getting high and burst through the door demanding a bag of dope and a syringe. I can't remember her name, but she had a pink mohawk and was adamant about me not damaging her only syringe. Of course the needle broke off in my arm as soon as I tried to push down the plunger, and I ended up having to stumble back to town to try and find a rig.

I remember standing back out front of a packed Tinker Street It was summertime and everyone loved to party till four a.m., but there was not one fucking junky there. I remembered that I had hidden a rig at my friend Paris's place right down the hill, so I charged head first through yet another door where a few rogues were getting ready to go to the Joyous Lake, the only other bar in town. I didn't say a word, just jumped up onto the sink and scrambled my hand around the top of the dusty spider egg infested dish cabinet, and there it was right where I left it a year prior. I fell off the counter and sat on the couch that didn't seem to have one spring in it, dumped the broken syringe into a spoon, and drew it up with this dusty, dull ass poker that I hadn't used since Reagan was president. It was one of those syringes that had been used so many times that the numbers were rubbed off. That was always a painful hit. Everyone had taken off to the bar but Jed, who for some reason stayed back to make sure I was okay. I sharpened the needle with the striker of a matchbook and hit a vein on the first try. I felt my dick get a little hard when the blood squirmed its way into the syringe, and the next thing I remember is hearing Jed ask if I was all right. He kept saying it really fast over and over, but the more he said it, the farther away his voice got. It was like someone was holding my head under water and I couldn't lift up to breathe, but I wasn't scared. It felt fucking like I was entering heaven.

When we were kids we used to sit in Scottie's driveway after school and get stoned in his car while his parents were at work. One time his neighbor who was a couple of years older than us was home visiting from Venice Beach, California, and hopped into the back seat to join us. That day he told us that if we loved pot, we would really love heroin, because heroin was super pot. That was the day that a little poppy seed was planted in the back of my head.

I woke up to Paris sitting on my chest slapping me in the face as hard as he could. Everyone who'd gone to the bar was now back in the apartment, yelling my name and crying, poor Jed's ginger-freckled face was bright red and covered in tears. I had no clue what happened but apparently I was dead, like not-breathing-turning-blue kinda dead. I guess Jed had run up to the Joyous Lake after not being able to wake me up and they all came back and tried to revive me. I wasn't coming around right away and Paris called 911, because among all the screaming and crying, there were police banging on the door as I started to sit up. The scumbags I hung out with cared more about their friends being alive than getting in trouble. We weren't complete pieces of shit, thank God, most junkies would have just dragged me behind the apartment and threw me into the stream. The cops came in and helped me up. Paris told them I was epileptic and hit my head having a seizure, but when they asked me what kind of medication I was taking I had to come clean and tell them I was really drunk and slipped. They asked me if I wanted to go to the hospital, I said no, and that was that—off they went to go fuck high school girls or jerk off in each other's mouths or whatever they did when no one was looking.

MONSTER IN THE WATER

WITHIN THE WEEK I WAS right back onto that hamster wheel, with the glorious ritual consuming my life once again. I didn't have a job anymore, I moved out of the place I was renting, and was now either crashing on Tony's pile of dirty clothes or a leaf pile in the woods.

The silver lining of this dark cloud is that I did make a new connection with the best dope in town, and I was the only one who knew about him. He'd just gotten out of prison and had full-blown AIDS, and I don't know why I told you that. It has nothing to do with anything except for I was a little freaked out about the AIDS thing because I used to shoot up in his bathroom. It was the perfect situation. If I bought four bags from him, he gave me one for free, plus I was getting them for twenty bucks and charging everyone else twenty-five, so every trip I would get two free bags for myself. I didn't have to pay for dope anymore, and the shit was so fucking good that everyone wanted it. Since I was the only one who could get it, I now had a new job and would show up on the green every morning around eleven and collect money from the sick and get a ride out to his place. I never had to worry about running out of dope...ever.

I didn't have to do shit like steal quarters from Scott and Kelly's bedroom laundry jug anymore, either. There's nothing more humiliating than having to steal from your best friends and then hitchhike down the road in the middle of the day holding your pants up with one hand and your thumb out on the other because each pocket is seven pounds. Not having to worry about kicking or money was a welcomed inconvenience for both me and them.

There was one kid in particular who would come and pick me up every morning at Tony's and buy enough dope that I could hold myself over for the entire day. He would steal money from his graveyard shift job at the gas station and then come bang on Tony's window when he got off. After we became friends, I would go there at night to shoot dope in the bathroom and eat all the Entenmann's cakes and ice cream for free. I would do shit like steal disposable cameras off the wall and then come back the next day and return them for cash to the day shift guy. I was fucking killing it in the dope game.

When customers paid for gas with a card, my dude would overcharge the cards like five or ten dollars each. When we had enough he would hand me the money and the keys to his car, and off I would go to the AIDS guy's house about two miles down the road. I would cop, come back, and get high until the end of his shift, and he would either take me back to Tony's or sneak me into his parents' house.

One gorgeous summer night I took his car to go cop but had been doing a little extra heavy sedating that day. I think I was popping Klonopin or something, oh, and the AIDS guy had also brought back some crack from his last run into the city and threw me a few vials for being such a loyal, committed customer. I think I was making this guy happier than he was making me with all the business I was bringing in. The road to the AIDS guy was tricky at night, all the backroads up there are—no streetlights, super dark, very winding with jagged turns, and at some point the road flowed right against the edge of some body of water. I'm not sure if it was a pond or a lake or what, all I know is that I had shot a full bag at AIDS guy's house right before getting into the car with a fully packed crack pipe, and I really shouldn't have been behind the wheel of anything.

The next thing I remember is driving down the road steering with my knee so I could use both my hands to smoke the rock. "Lightning Crashes" by Live was playing on the home of rock and roll 101.5 WPDH and my favorite part was coming up, those of you who have seen Corey Taylor's acoustic show know exactly what part I am talking about. But right before the part came on, my knee slipped off the wheel and I swerved into some bushes. I didn't even know what happened. The car just stopped. I tried to put it in reverse and get the fuck out of there, but every time I pressed my foot onto the gas pedal I would hear the sound of water splashing. So, yeah, I wasn't in the bushes—I was in the water, and quickly sinking nose first. The more I jammed my foot on the pedal the more my leg would submerge into water, and I finally jumped out.

I hitched a ride to town to try and find someone with a truck and maybe a chain with a hook or something. My plan was to have someone pull it out of the water and I would clean it up real quick and take it back before anyone knew what had happened. I tumbled around the bars asking for help but all I got was a belt because apparently my pants were at my knees (I had taken mine off to shoot up and forgot it at AIDS guy's house). I don't remember the rest of that night, but I most likely finished the crack and passed out in the woods.

The next day I ran into my old roommate on the green who was now driving the local taxi. He picked me up to get him a bag and started laughing hysterically when I got in the car. I asked him what he was chuckling about in the rear view mirror, and he proceeded to tell a story about how he went to the gas station the night before to meet me and was smoking a cigarette with a dude out front wondering what was taking me so long, when all of asudden the dude's car drove past hooked up to the back of a tow truck and was pouring out water with weeds coming out of all the places.

I got chased out of Tony's by the cops that next morning. He had not lived there in weeks and I was just squatting until someone finally came and told me to go. I wandered aimlessly around town watching all my normal friends drive by shaking their heads in disappointment. I cared so much what they thought of me, but I couldn't fucking stop.

LOVE YOUR MOTHER LIKE YOU LOVE YOUR HEROIN

Yup, here I was again back at Mom's—except this time there were no doctors or nurses. My stepfather, Rick, had moved back in, Nani was dead, and Aimee was now in high school, and here I was still doing the same old shit. But, hey, this time I was dead fucking serious about getting my shit together.

I woke up on the second morning of my arrival to an empty house. I was sick, so the entire house smelled weird and was mildly vibrating. I crawled up the steps to try and force a bowl of Cap'n Crunch down my throat; the sugar always helped a little and I wanted to lay on the cold kitchen tile for a little bit to soothe my aching cheeks. For some reason Cody's phone number kept running through my head. This was the pre–cell phone era, so you actually had phone numbers stored in your memory. I only ever called Cody once from a diner in Manhattan a very long time ago, and I hadn't seen him or Ben in forever, so to have this phone number bouncing through my skull in the same way that people count sheep to try and go to sleep was really fucking strange. Every second that passed the numbers got bigger and bigger in my head. Goddammit, man, I knew I couldn't do it again, not to myself, especially not to my mother and my poor little sister. There was no way for me to get down there anyway, right? FUCK!! I just needed to be strong and hold on. I needed this shit to fucking end already. I heard those losers in NA when they said that this feeling would pass, so I laid on the floor and waited. I waited and waited for the feeling to pass, and the next thing I remember is the phone being in my hand and Cody was on the other line saying, "Wassup, Jay! Ben's on his way up here now, you comin'!?"

What were the fucking chances that at the exact moment I decided to call this fucking guy he actually picked up the phone *and* Ben was on his way up to score?

I can't even tell you how soothing it was to hear Cody's voice and find out that Ben was still in the game. Knowing that actually made me less sick. I immediately started scheming on how I was going to get down there from the middle of nowhere Rockland County with no car and no money, get dope, then get back up to the house before anyone got home from work or school. It was about forty-five miles away, so I had to be smart and act fast. Unfortunately, I was only good at one of those things.

Mom's old red Jetta was sitting in the driveway, waiting for my sister to get her license, so I scoured every drawer in the house looking for the keys but couldn't find them. I fucking looked everywhere. I looked through the window of the car thinking maybe they were up in the visor or something, but nothing. My mother probably had them hidden in her purse because she knew I would eventually pull some bullshit like this.

I was smack dab in the center of a horseshoe cul-de-sac that had a declining hill to the left of the house. It was steep enough that I figured if I could somehow get into the car and roll it down the hill, I could pop the stick shift into second gear and be on my way to Cody and Ben in no time. I had to be fast though. If Ben split before I got to Harlem, I would have no way of getting a hold of him, and I didn't have any money to get anything on my own, so I'd be fucked. I grabbed a coat hanger from the closet, went to the car, and pulled the lock. I popped the emergency brake and pushed it up to the edge of the driveway, cranking the wheel as far as I could to the left, giving it one good push off as I jumped in and slammed the door. Now, mind you, just twenty minutes before I could barely crawl up the steps for cereal, and here I was pushing a four-thousand-pound car up a driveway. The mind is a terrible thing to waste.

My adrenaline was on another level. I jammed my foot on the clutch and tried to pop it into gear. Attempt one, fail. Second try, nothing. Now I was picking up speed and getting closer to the curb. I gave it one last shot and screamed into the windshield as I felt the front tires bounce off the curb. The car stopped and there I was, stuck at the bottom of the cul-de-sac. There was no fucking way I could push the car back up to the house by myself—it was too far away—and I had already wasted way too much time on this. I couldn't worry about my parents freaking out, and I had to figure something else out immediately, so I left the car where it was and ran back into the house to call a taxi. I went into my mother's bedroom and grabbed two gold plated watches out of the jewelry box on the dresser and gave them to the cab driver, telling him they were real, and that I would replace them for cash once we got to Harlem. I also gave him my expired driver's license. It took a minute, but he reluctantly agreed and started driving.

Holy fuck what a relief to finally be on my way.

Cody gave me his girlfriend's address and told me to whistle when I got to the front of the building, so I had the taxi drop me off on the opposite block and told him to wait while I ran up and got the money. I went into a building and snuck out a side door running around the corner unnoticed. As soon as I got to the corner I whistled and this scrawny Black woman poked her toothless head covered in a red bandana out of a window and tossed me down a set of keys, yelling the apartment number. I quickly ran inside before the cab driver realized I wasn't coming back.

The apartment was a tropical climate, to say the least. I had just run up five flights and was reeeeally starting to feel that there was no dope in my system and got super dizzy. The apartment smelled like hot grape soda, which she was actually swigging from a two-liter bottle, but not before pouring a teaspoon of sugar into the spout before each sip. No wonder she had no teeth. She was absolutely one-hundred-percent the textbook definition of a crackhead. Cody was getting the drugs and Ben was still on his way. I was relieved that I had made it, and everything was going to be fine. But the weird thing was that I wasn't even thinking about all the shit I had just pulled at my mother's house, like I was so focused on sticking a needle in my arm that not one bit of what I had done was even a thought in my head.

There was an episode of *CHiPs* on the little black and white TV, so I slunk down on the couch and took a deep breath trying to focus on that until they got back. A man screaming and honking his horn in the distance got louder, but would then disappear, and then come back a few minutes later, then disappear again. That poor taxi driver must have circled that block for at least an hour looking for me while the crackheads sat at the window laughing maniacally at him. Eventually the honking stopped, and the boys came home. I hugged everyone and ran into the bathroom. It was so tiny that my knees hit the pipes under the sink when I sat down to shoot up on the toilet. The old clanking heater next to me felt like it was taking a layer of skin off the side of my leg as I got myself together. I lightly brushed some cold water against my face to rid myself of the sweat while the speedball I had just injected made the world right again. Everything smelled better, and all I wanted was a strawberry shortcake ice cream bar. It was a quick meeting and Ben had to head back home, I went with him even though his mother wanted me nowhere near him and called my mom. She was at work in the city, so I told her that I was having a hard time being alone, so Ben came to pick me up for lunch. She was so happy that I was asking people for help and agreed to come get me when she was finished. So I shot up one more time at Ben's and went downstairs to wait for my mother before his mother came home and freaked out.

It had been a couple of days since I had done any drugs, so I was really fucking high. I couldn't really stop my eyeballs from shaking and I was sweating through my undershirts, but I played it off as well as I could when I got in the car, and even though I had done this kind of shit around my mother before, she wasn't really aware of the signs to look for in someone who was high.

The conversation about my fake day was going pretty smoothly until her cell phone rang. The tone in her voice changed immediately and these were the next words out of her mouth...

"WHAT?

"YOU FOUND THE CAR WHERE?

"WHAT TAXI?!

"GOLD WATCHES?!! I DON'T HAVE ANY GOLD WATCHES!?"

"COPS?!

"RICKY, WHAT THE FUCK ARE YOU TALKING ABOUT!!?"

She hung up the phone and didn't say a word, she was so mad I don't even think a muscle moved in her face the entire time. She drove straight to Nyack hospital, pulling up right in front of the emergency room doors, and said, "I have no idea who you are, you're not my son. Get the fuck out of my car."

I walked in and sat down in a chair opposite a heavy Puerto Rican lady in a bright, flowered shirt behind the plexiglass. She shoved a bunch of papers through the hole for me to sign, which I did, and then I went into the bathroom to shoot up the last loaded rig I had hidden in my sock. I looked down to spit into the toilet because shooting coke makes the salivary glands erupt like a motherfucker, and noticed a giant syringe with a blue tip on the floor... It was the exact same rig that I had used to shoot up at the model's apartment on that New Year's Eve in 1995.

Poetic? A message from the NA gods? Sure, why the fuck not. I definitely needed to take this as a sign that it was time to get my shit together.

But here comes the sad part, ready?

I don't even remember who I called the next morning from the payphone in the detox to come get me. I feel like it was K, but the timeline doesn't match up. Who the fuck cares anyway? The point is that I only lasted twelve hours before I was out the door again. Only this time I had to MacGyver my way out of the facility because it was all locked up from the outside, so I followed the janitor as he was leaving and stuffed a napkin into the exit door. I waited until the coast was clear and snuck out to meet whoever came to get me, and back upstate I went.

THE RAT

AN OLD FRIEND GAVE me a napkin full of little blue pills that I was popping like M&M's to keep from getting sick because the AIDS guy hadn't answered his phone in two days. It was mid-February and no one was around and the town was dry as a bone. I tried to cop from one of the nickel-and-dime dealers that I could only deal with if it was an absolute last resort because of his mental health issues, but when I came up five dollars short on a bag he screamed at me and kicked me out of his car with nothing, making me walk two miles back to town. I was feeling like I should have never left California, and it definitely had to be the reason everything was so fucked up.

All I had to keep me warm were these little blue pills and a zippered hoodie twice my size that I got from the free store. I had been roaming around town earlier that day trying to figure out who I could take something from so I could have some money just in case AIDS guy picked up his phone, but it had been long enough to where I figured he was probably sitting in jail by now. I had cashed in all my favors anyway. No one, I mean literally no one, wanted anything to do with me. It was so bad that after an old friend's little sister had picked me up hitchhiking on her way home from school and dropped me off on the green one day, she got pulled over right after so the cops could tell her to stay away from me.

Detox, Aunt Marie's, Mom's, Scott and Kelly's, all that shit was off the table. Los Angeles didn't want me either. I was completely on my own and incapable of doing anything but robbing people I loved to survive. Earlier that day, I walked into a head shop in town that I used to work at and stuffed something in the lock of the back door hoping to come back after they closed and steal a bunch of stuff to barter for dope. The woman who owned the shop treated me like family when I worked there. I pierced for her at Woodstock '94, right before I left for LA. She and her mother would let me crash when I had no place to stay (before I got all scummy and thievey); she fed me, consoled me, gave me confidence when I needed it, and I just took a huge shit on all of it because all I cared about was getting high. When I went back that night the door was locked, and the napkin I used to stuff the lock was resting on the doorknob waiting for me. I got so freaked out and thought they were watching me from the bushes, so I took off with my hood over my head but came back snooping again like twenty minutes later.

I was alone in the dark shadows of the village green trying to avoid the snow. It was around four a.m. when I went behind that same head shop to take a piss and noticed that the window to the pizzeria was open a crack. I was freezing and hungry, so I pushed up the window and crawled inside to get warm and have a snack. I worked at a deli in New Jersey a few years back, so when I saw the register, I knew there might be some money in it for when they opened in the morning. I found the key underneath and popped it open, finding a bunch of fives, singles, and quarters. Jackpot!

I grabbed a bottle of grape soda out of the cooler and sat at one of the tables by the window as I watched the cops patrol through town. I was way too clouded on pills to think rationally about anything. They parked at the edge of the green and sat there for what seemed like an eternity before finally pulling away. I grabbed the money and a portable phone and crawled back out the window into the cold. I thought to myself, if this window was open, how many others in town were?

I wasn't a criminal. I was for sure a menacing drug addict, but breaking and entering? This was a whole new level for me. I didn't really count stealing from my family and friends as being a thief. I was oblivious to what my world had become and was so disconnected from everything and everyone, except heroin and anyone who could give it to me, that I barely even talked anymore. I could go an entire day without saying more than five words.

The rest of that night was spent sneaking around town, climbing through unlocked windows, and kicking open doors. I was weighed down with morning change and my shoes were stuffed with fives and singles. I had collected a little over a hundred bucks.

It was a little after five a.m. and I could see the sun attempting to pierce through the grayish black sky that had been providing me cover for most of the night. I had one more store to hit, and then was going to bail into the woods until I could make a few calls to try and get some dope. Hopefully AIDS guy got bailed out by now.

The last store I was going to hit had what I thought was a stained-glass window, but when I tapped on it I quickly realized it was some type of plastic. I could see that the register was right on the other side of the window through the yellow part of the stain, so this was gonna be a piece of cake. All I had to do was make a hole in the plastic with my lighter, stick my hand through, grab the money, and bounce—so that's exactly what I did. The little key was already in the register, all I had to do was turn it to Z and pop it open. But as I reached for the register, I tripped a silent alarm triggered by lasers, which created a massive strobe light with a siren so loud they probably heard it in Jersey.

The police station was right down the road, so I had to abort quickly. There was a big parking lot behind the store that I ducked into but could only get as far as the dumpster by the hardware store that K used to work in before cop cars started screeching into all the entrances. The only thing I could do was crouch down behind it and wait patiently for these fucking nuisances to finish their bullshit and go back to jerking off in a speed trap. I could see them, but they couldn't see me. I watched them mull around the window, flashing their lights all around the ground looking for clues. All I had to do was be patient until the coast was clear and then walk back into town like nothing had happened, but the lighter the sky became, the more nervous I got. Dawn was my enemy at this point and I just needed these fucking assholes to stop fucking up my vibe. My knees were hurting from crouching, my hands were freezing, and I was getting sick again.

After the longest thirty minutes of my life, when it looked like they were all starting to get back in their cars and I could make the great escape, the dumpster shook drastically like something inside it exploded, and began to float magically into the air. I thought I was hallucinating, but then realized that a garbage truck had come to empty the fucking thing! It was just my luck that right then at that very moment, it just happened to be garbage day. I looked directly into the driver's eyes as he yelled, "HE'S OVER HERE!!!" So I jumped up and took off running, the only chance I had was to somehow make it into the woods, but I only made it to The Joyous Lake before the cops had their guns drawn behind me. I dropped to my knees and put my hands in the air like they told me. I hung my head in shame as the handcuffs tightly gripped my wrists, they were so cold. I was placed into the back of the car and taken to the police station, where I was thrown into a tiny cell and handcuffed to a wall. This was the same place K sat when she was crying on the phone to me to come get her dog. I sat there staring through the bars, imagining that the piles of papers on the desk were the bundles of dope they got busted with.

I had been there a few hours and was becoming very sick. The blue pills had worn off, I hadn't shot dope in a few days, and the cops were pointing and laughing at me every time they walked by making stupid comments like they'd just arrested Nicky Barnes. I wanted to fucking die, and even though I was sick and in dire straits, I still felt superior to these idiots. I didn't really have a problem with cops in general, just these particular cops. The chief poked his head in front of the bars right at the height of my jones, and with his big fat head and spacious brown teeth started dramatically saying shit like, "Ya want that dope, don't ya, Jason? You want that dope. I can see it in your bloodshot little eyes…"

He was right. I wanted that fucking dope. I needed that fucking dope.

Around nine a.m., all the business owners were getting to their shops and finding out that they had been robbed, so the phones started ringing off the hook. One guy came in who I heard through the wall with a very angry tone and said, "Did Jason Rappise do this?!" (My real last name.)

I like to think that I'm the reason the town started locking their doors and putting in alarm systems.

They uncuffed me and brought me to the detective's office in the back. The cop who had been watching me be a fuck up for years was taking down my info. He looked at my slouched over sorry ass and said, "You know you really fucked up here, right, Jason? You're looking at doing a substantial amount of time…"

That was the moment I realized I wasn't going to get to do dope that day, and that was definitely not okay with me. I needed a plan, and the only thing I could think of to get out of this situation was to throw the guy that kicked me out of his car because I didn't have enough money for a bag of dope under the bus hard. In my sick, fiending mind he deserved this, and just like that, in a dope sick moment of panic, I became a rat.

I knew that the cops had their eye on this guy, so when I mentioned possibly giving him to them for immunity, it definitely piqued their interest. I thought that they would give me money, let me go up to his house and cop, I would do a bag while I was there to get well, and then they would go up there after I left and bust him.

Sounds easy enough, right?

They agreed to make the deal happen, but then told me that the only way it could be done was if the DEA was involved. I had to wait two hours for an agent to come down from Albany. They wanted me to go up to the dude's house with this agent, get him to sell her dope, and come back to the station with it. Then, and only then, would I be a free man.

The sickness had completely taken over and was I obviously not giving a shit whose life I destroyed, but I was still absolutely terrified. This dude was paranoid as fuck, and I knew in my heart that there was no way in hell this was going to work. I was just trying to buy myself some time and get high before I went to jail. I didn't really think about the endgame.

So I'm standing outside the door smoking a cigarette when this brand-new shiny, white Mustang with a beige convertible roof pulls down the driveway. This hot young black cop gets out wearing a sweater jacket and tight blue jeans, looking exactly like the one from 21 Jump Street. I knew right then that there was no way this was going to work, but it was either she came with me or we didn't go. Blah blah blah, we get in the car and start driving toward dude's place, some small talk ensues on the way, and by small talk I mean her saying shit cops say, and me staring out the window not being able to blink my eyes because all I'm trying to do is not vomit in my lap from fear. There are cops following us closely in undercover cars that will stop at the end of dude's road in case something happens. The closer we get, the more damp I become. I can't believe this is my fucking life now, when just a short time ago I was almost living out my rock star fantasy in Hollywood, California.

My heart is blasting the inside of my chest like a fucking jackhammer. We came around the bend and I saw him sitting on the front porch with another guy I wasn't too fond of. He stood up immediately as we pulled into his driveway and he started flailing his arms and charging toward me, screaming, "Who the fuck is this!!??" and "What the fuck is going on!?!?" over and over.

I got out of the car and attempted to tell him in an extremely shaky voice that she was my drug dealer friend from Albany who came down to try and cop because it was dry up there, but this made him even angrier. He started screaming for us to get off his property while pushing me back toward the car. She tried to get all ghetto by yelling, "Come on, sugar, I don't need this bullllshit!" and we got in the car and sped off.

I couldn't believe what had happened; what the fuck had I just done? I could never show my face in town again. But that didn't even matter because the deal went south and now I was going to jail. I was fucked.

They took me directly into the courthouse where I stood handcuffed between the defendant and prosecutor tables waiting for Judge Engel to come in and send me away. It felt like an hour had gone by before he walked through the door. I picked my head up as he sat and we went through the all rise bullshit motions. And then, out of nowhere, he says, "Well, Jason, I can't believe I'm about to do this, but you're released on your own recognizance. You are free to go, but you have to go back up to dude's house by yourself tomorrow and get us what we want…"

The officer uncuffed me from behind, my hands fell to my sides, and that was that.

I was fucking free to go.

No, I'm not joking.

They let me just walk the fuck out like nothing happened and expected me to go back up to dude's and buy dope like I wasn't just there trying to ruin his life with an undercover. These were some of the dumbest people on the planet.

It had to be midafternoon by this time, and I was so disoriented and blown away by what had just happened that I completely forgot about robbing all the stores and started walking right through town. As I passed all the store fronts, I noticed that everyone was standing on the stoops of their stores and looking at me. I swear to God, I had completely blocked out everything until that moment, and then it all came crashing in. I heard someone in the distance say, "How the fuck is he walking around right now?" so I quickly dipped behind that last building I tried to rob and headed down a back road to the payphone at Grand Union. I called my old roommate in the taxi, and he pulled up five minutes later and told me to get in the backseat and lie down because I wasn't allowed to hang out with him either.

The first thing I did when I laid down was grab the car phone and call the AIDS guy. This was all his fucking fault, as far as I was concerned. If he would have just answered his phone none of this would have happened. The relief in my voice when he actually answered was one of almost paralyzing ecstasy. He apologized, telling me he was stuck in the city and just got back, and that it was cool for me to come up, so I hung up the phone and told the old roomie I would give him a bag if he drove me up there. But the guy that I just tried to rat out had called him to ask if he knew the black girl that I was with. My old roomie told me that if I wanted him to drive up there I had to give him three bags for taking the risk.

I was close with the old roomie and always felt like I could trust him. He was the guy I went to in the first book when I was riddled with stage fright before the first Beast show at Tinker Street and who got me stoned and calmed me down with a breathing exercise.

So on the way to get the dope, I told him everything.

One very important thing I forgot to mention was that the cops were so fucking stupid they never checked my pockets or made me take off my shoes, and I still had all the money. What I wasn't sure of was how fast the word was going to spread about what I had just done. The word was already out about the robberies, but who the fuck knew how many other people dude had called about me possibly being a rat. What if AIDS guy had heard about what happened and was just setting me up? Luckily I was more sick than scared, and not going up there wasn't an option.

He was waiting at the door for me when I got there, opening it before I could knock and staring at me blankly. For a second I thought I was a dead man, I was just waiting for the gun to come up from his side. But instead, he opened the door all the way and shook my hand, saying he was sorry once again. My heart sank back into my chest and I bought as much shit as I could, got high in his bathroom, and ran back to the car. I sat in the back seat and let everything that just happened soak into my body like a fucking plague.

I had just committed like seven felonies and become a rat, two things I thought would never happen in my life. I didn't know what to do, but one thing was for sure: I had to get the fuck out of town, and I had to do so immediately. These morons were expecting me to go back up there in the morning and if I didn't come back with anything, they would for sure be looking for me the next morning. But where the fuck was I going to go?

Robbing my grandmother blind had kinda put a damper on my family helping me out ever again, but I had no other choice but to try. It was getting dark out and everyone who wanted my head on a stick had gone home for the day, so I had the old roomie drop me off in the same parking lot I got busted in and snuck into Taco Juan's (one of the places I tried to break into but couldn't) to call my mother collect from the payphone. She was angry, worried, and not stoked to come get me but begrudgingly said that her and my stepfather would drive up.

The next phone call I made was to the AIDS guy. I told him I needed a front because I was going to my parents' to kick and asked him to put a bunch of dope in a suitcase and meet me at the end of his road. When my mom and Rick pulled around the green, I ran from the alley I was hiding in and jumped into the back seat of the car. It was dead silent as we pulled away and headed to the thruway, but I had to break that silence and tell them that I needed to grab a suitcase full of my stuff from a friend on the way. Balls of steel guided me as I directed them to my dope dealer's street and pulled up next to a waiting truck. He threw the suitcase out the window at me and sped off, kicking dirt and rocks up at me while I stood there wincing.

Not a word was spoken the whole ride back to Rockland County. When we got to the house, I went straight into my sister's room to see what AIDS guy had left for me in the suitcase. I was expecting at the very least a few bags and a syringe, but all that was in the suitcase was a prescription bottle holding two methadone pills, and that was it. It would barely take care of the next day. Oddly enough I didn't freak out, I knew it was over.

I laid on my sister's bed, turned on her little TV, and stared into the light like a catatonic dog while reruns of *Beverly Hills 90210* polluted my brain just enough to make me forget about what just happened.

My sister came home, so I moved onto that shitty pullout that I almost died on in the living room and tried to enjoy the last night of decent sleep I would get for who the fuck knows how long. That poor little girl watched me wither into just about nothing since I was twenty years old—but, hey, she never touched the shit so at least it amounted to something good.

The next day while I was in the shower, my stepdad opened my suitcase and saw that it was empty. He didn't ask any questions, he just told me to get dressed because he was taking me to Ross for clothes. I popped a methadone pill and off we went. Later that night, while I was lying on the couch waiting for the second pill to kick in, I got a call from the old roomie. He was sitting in his cab on the green watching a long line of cop cars make their way up the mountain toward the house that I had just ruined my life at. I guess since I jumped ship they decided to go up on their own, but what they didn't realize because they are fucking idiots was that right after I left dude's yard that day he probably cleaned out his house, which is why they got nothing but a scale and some empty baggies from what I heard. I still feel terrible that they raided his parents' house with guns and dogs though. I never wanted any of that shit to happen; I just thought I was gonna go up and get some dope and then he'd go to jail for a month or something. What was the harm in that?

The old roomie asked me for my mom's address so he could write me a letter. I didn't think too much of it, but later I found out that he tried to sell it to dude for dope.

That's some cold shit. "I know it was you, Fredo. You broke my heart..."

NYACK RECOVERY CENTER

THE NEXT MORNING, I WOKE up terrified of my own shadow, and when I get scared, I run. So, what better place to run to than the only place left? Rehab. I was sick, the cops were looking for me, and it was only a matter of time until they made it to my mom's house. I was finished in every sense of the word. I also knew that by making it look like I was trying to do the right thing on my own and entering a treatment facility that I would get at least half my sentence cut. This was my third or fourth time in this particular facility, and I was never able to make it out of the detox. Luckily there was a bed available because it was the dead of fucking winter in upstate New York, and back then the laws were so lax that you could go to detox like twelve times a year if you wanted, so when it got cold all the homeless junkies would run there. You had a better shot of getting an all-access pass to a Black Sabbath reunion than ever getting a warm bed in a state-run rehab in the middle of February.

I was so fucking wiped out from ruining my life that I slept for like forty-eight hours straight. I woke up in a detox bed to the most horrible stench coming from a pair of work boots that had been neatly placed next to a closed pink curtain that was barely muffling a rambunctious snore in the next bed over. It smelled so bad I felt like there had to be maggots somewhere in the area. Turned out to be some weird homeless guy that used to shoot embalming fluid in the basement of a funeral home surrounded by all the dead bodies, which is where the giant vein on the right side of his forehead came from. I only know that information because that was the first thing he told me after he woke up besides his name, which was Al.

That's right. For the whole rest of the trip there, his name was Al Coholic.

All I could think of every time I saw him was how the mortician wouldn't have to do any work if he overdosed and died.

These were the types of people that were in my life now.

I was proud of myself for finally making it into the rehab, I still spent the first few days beating myself up for being a twenty-six-year-old man child who seemed to have an enormous amount of trouble getting his shit together, which normally would make me run out of there as fast as I could to repeat the cycle all over again. But instead of leaving, I would pull a chair up to the big fish tank in the main group room and stare at my reflection in the glass for hours. The antennas of the exotic fish would sway back and forth hypnotically while the light reflected all kinds of colors off their scales. It would calm my tears so I could breathe.

My counselor's name was Steve. He always seemed to be wearing a yellow button-down shirt with brown pleated pants, and he had his hair cut and feathered like he had been married for too long and given up on life. Steve would remind me daily that if I didn't get with the program, I would always end up in a way less fun place than I was in right now. He would high five me in the hallway in passing every day and tell me how great I was doing, almost making me feel glad to be alive. It was either be a team player or go to prison, so I started showing up to groups early and setting up the chairs. I would be the first to raise my hand and participate whether I believed what these minimum wage, cheap-ass-suit-wearing, snake oil salesmen were saying or not. I didn't even care that all I was getting was that shitty yellow pill at bedtime that never put me to sleep. I started sleeping at night—an hour here, two or three hours there—and before I knew it I was sleeping all the way through the night.

The cops found out where I was. To my surprise, they were just glad that I was in a treatment center. That was a huge weight lifted off of me, and even though I knew I was eventually going to have to deal with them, right now I could just focus on getting better.

The air in the smoke room was so thick you could slice it with your finger. Every corner had a shitty chair upholstered in freezing cold vinyl with old dirty tape covering the rips and burn marks up and down the arms. Standing ashtrays overflowed onto the shitty red carpet as the tobacco-stained walls and buzzing fluorescent lights really enhanced the entire smoking experience. I couldn't spend enough time in that room...

The only contact we had with the outside world other than seeing family on visiting day was when people from the meetings would come speak. Every night at seven we would have a meeting with a speaker. I would always hope it would be a hot girl so I could masturbate about her when I went to bed. It had gotten so bad that I was jerking off about the sixty-five-year-old Jamaican nurse at the front desk who gave me my sleeping pill every night. I hadn't had or wanted to have sex with anyone in well over a year and was now a walking hard-on as the dope wore off. I was jerking off in the shower so much that I still get a hard on when it rains.

Before I knew it, my time at the rehab had come to an end. This was my very first time completing a program, and even though I did it because I would have gone to jail otherwise, I was still pretty proud of myself. I was so excited to sit in the final group where they go around the room and tell you what a dirty scumbag asshole you were when you first got there but now you're a butterfly pissing strawberry jelly into everyone's mouth as they send you back into the soiled journey from whence you came.

Mom picked me up exactly where she dropped me off, and off we went back to the Stony Point, the scene of the car-stuck-at-the-end-of-the-road crime. Mom was happy I was clean, but worried I wasn't going to last long, and with very good reason. I never lasted very long. She had that "Oh my junky failure of a son is gonna give it another shot so I better stay positive and hope he doesn't disappear again" look on her face as I sang along blissfully to classic rock songs in the passenger seat while waving my hand out the car window through the air pretending it was Superman like I used to do when I was a kid.

CCP

I COULDN'T WAIT TO get back to Mom's and start my fresh new life in Rockland County. I was so excited about it that I had completely forgotten I was a wanted man. I was quickly reminded as we pulled into the cul-de-sac and I saw the cops waiting in the driveway. I gave Mom a hug and threw my bag into the back of the police car, driving back upstate with them so I could be sentenced to two to seven years. I had a bunch of second-degree breaking-and-entering charges, fleeing from police, hindering an investigation. I don't even remember all the shit they were throwing at me. Judges don't take kindly to runners, but since I had run to rehab and was obviously trying to do the right thing, I was hoping for a little leniency. Luckily, while I was lounging in the dorm in my bright orange jumpsuit, sleeping on my shitty sneakers, a new program for drug addicts that I apparently qualified for came across my plate.

I was lucky enough to be one of the thirty who they thought might actually have a shot at rehabilitation and was put in this little building right next to the jail.

We got to wear regular clothes, order pizza, and watch movies on Friday nights. We were allowed to smoke cigarettes and use the payphones whenever we wanted, too. It was definitely more like rehab than jail, except we didn't get to order pizza, watch movies, or use phones in rehab—so it was actually better. The "guards" were regular dudes from the area, not corrections officers. They were my age and would come in hungover, talking about how they thought they might have gotten laid the night before but didn't remember. I wanted to be like them so fucking bad, but there was no fucking way I would be able to have a life like that outside of the walls I was temporarily trapped behind. As soon as I was released from this shithole, I was going to have to lose all my teeth and go right back to NA.

We all slept in one giant dorm room. Blacks, whites, Puerto Ricans, crackheads, bank robbers, department store kleptos, all of us snoring, farting, and phlegming it up every minute of every day and night for six months straight. Real cream of the crop in there, I tell ya. Some of those guys had me laughing so hard I would almost pee myself. One time we were all woken up by the paramedics because one of the inmates thought that the foam in the mop bucket looked like the head of a beer, so he fucking drank it. That's where addiction takes some people, drinking dirty bleach water that was just used to clean the bathroom in a men's county jail. I feel like if you're that deep in it, you may as well just kill yourself.

We had access to two payphones and could use them basically anytime we wanted. There was nobody in my circle anxiously awaiting to accept my collect calls, but I knew that there was one person in the world who would always listen to me, always love me, and always make me feel like I wanted to feel, so I called the operator (again) and tracked down her number the exact same way that I did at Jeff's apartment in Los Angeles a couple of years prior. Within minutes I had that sweet Southern tone melting my heart once again. Bobbi's voice was like Coltrane on vinyl and always there when I needed it, and I really needed it. It only took a little begging before she once again caved and took me back. God, her mother couldn't stand me.

I hadn't seen her since the fiasco at the apartment on Wilton, so she sent me some recent pictures that were sprayed with perfume. When those pictures showed up I couldn't believe how hot she was. I mean, she was always hot, but holy fuck did she bud up into a most perfect flower. I was so fucking stoked to show all the guys in the dorm who my new girlfriend was. I hung the pictures on the ceiling of my bunk and would imagine the fantasy that she told me she had of us cruising through the warm summer nights in Dallas with the top down and the music cranked. Making out in the grass, splitting a milkshake, having a couple of kids. I don't know, maybe being a normal guy for once in my fucking life. One picture she sent was her as a young girl attached to a letter telling me that this was probably what our daughter would look like, and I was totally into it.

I must have written her like a hundred letters while I was in there, or maybe it was just a few and it felt like a hundred. Either way I got a response—so I had that going for me, which was always nice—and she never declined my collect calls. And even though I never spoke to her again once I got out of that shithole, because that was the kind of douchebag I was, I would like to thank you one last time for keeping me alive through the hardest time in my life, Bobbi Rodriguez. I appreciate you more than you think I do.

I was so scared and ashamed of what I had done to get into this place. I feared for my life and was very concerned that someone would get wind of it and beat the shit out of me in the showers for being a rat. I didn't know if I should get in front of the situation that could possibly arise and just tell everyone, or just hope it never got brought up and slink through doing my time unscathed and petrified. I eventually felt safe enough with the bank robber to tell him one late night outside smoking a cigarette, and he just shrugged it off as a "Well, junkies do that shit" kinda thing...so after that I didn't feel so bad about it.

I only ended up doing about four months of that program before I was released into the world and let out on good behavior with five years of felony probation. All I had to do was keep my nose clean for that long and everything would be fine. I wasn't a violent or malicious person; I was just a sad puppy that kept peeing on the rug. I didn't need to be locked up; I needed help. I went back to Mom's house smack dab in the middle of fall, which is beautiful but cold as fuck. The rule was the same as it was at Aunt Marie's: as long as I stayed sober and went to meetings, I was cool to stay there as long as I needed.

EXODUKES

INSTEAD OF DYING AT twenty-seven years of age like most of my "idols," I was given another chance. Not even another, I was just getting a chance *period*. I had never really had a life before and decided that the day I got out was the day I was going to start building a life for myself.

Mom fried some chicken cutlets in cornflake crumbs and served them up next to some mashed potatoes and frozen sweet corn—my favorite meal since I was a kid. The house smelled normal again, and it was nice to be able to climb the steps to the kitchen without wanting to fucking kill myself. I was overjoyed to not have to listen to dozens of dudes flatulate all day. Instead I could just pet the cats and hang on the couch while my sister's high school friends ogled over the newfound buffness I had created from doing tons of push-ups in lock up.

The time had come for me to make my first meeting as a free man. I stood in front of the bathroom mirror for about thirty minutes combing my hair strand by strand to get it Murray's pomade perfect. I had to look good in case there was a girl at the NA meeting that my mom was dropping me off at. I ripped the tags off my brand-new Dickies and pulled a fresh wifebeater out of the package. There was never any better feeling to me than putting on a brand-new wifebeater. I hooked the chain attached to my completely empty wallet, and off I went to get some new addictions I didn't even know I had yet.

Mommy dropped me off on a dark corner in front of this giant old church in Nyack and gave me two dollars for a cup of coffee. I could see the rehab I had squirmed in not too long ago up the street. Standing there, feeling the cold wet road underneath my thin Chucks, was my first moment of real gratitude. I was lucky to be able to stand up straight and take a deep breath without shitting myself or puking into my hands. Not being slave to the hypnotic hit me so fast that I almost fell over, while the sweet nectarous Nyack fall breeze cleansed my insides with each exhale.

I started to feel things like inspiration instead of failure, and pride instead of shame. It was such a trip. This was going to be my first true experience in recovery outside of a treatment center, the stingy amount of meetings I had attended in LA, and the candlelight biker meeting at some cabin up in Stony Point that my mom and her doctor boyfriend took me to, which left me with no real knowledge of what the program was all about. All I really knew was that a lot of people had been telling me I needed to go for a long fucking time.

The chill in the air bit the outline of my ears so hard it sent painful charges to the tips of my fingers. The dripping wet bushes soaked the sides of my pants as I walked down a narrow path toward the smell of cigarette smoke and failure. The louder the chattering got, the tighter my chest felt. I stopped right in the middle of the cloud for a second and looked around to soak it all in. No one approached me, I didn't approach anyone, I just stood there getting cottonmouth. People were talking about shooting heroin and laughing about getting arrested. I thought they were corny as fuck and spooked myself into turning around and walking out. I went and sat on the steps in front of the church and lit a cigarette, contemplating taking a walk around town and checking things out instead of hanging out with a bunch of sad old white people and one giant black dude. I was about to stand up when all of a sudden from across the street I heard a familiar NOFX song blaring from the inside of a blue Impala. The windows were rolled up and fogged so thick I couldn't see anything except a red cherry flare up every time whoever was in the driver's seat took a drag.

Henry would play NOFX all the time when we worked together at Tattoomania. He also gave me a poster of theirs to cover up the hole in my wall that Shitprints made with her head, and this is what drew me over to the car—so thank you, Henry.

I walked across the street wondering how this fucking guy wasn't deaf. Maybe he was and that's why the music was so loud. Also, smoking with the windows rolled up? This dude had to be a psycho, but I wasn't going into that meeting, and he was my only hope at this point. He started to roll down the window as I approached the car and smoke immediately engulfed my personal space, but not in a bad way. He made it look really cool, like even though I just put one out, I wanted to light another one—so I did.

He had dyed blue hair, a nose ring, and a huge scar down his cheek. But what really got my attention was the book in his lap. It was a big blue book with the letters NA stamped in gold on it. Maybe this meant that there might actually be cool people in recovery around these parts and not just a bunch of estranged mothers and fathers or bikers waiting to die from lung cancer at their auto body shops or whatever the fuck jobs sober people do. He turned down the music, told me his name was Rob, and after establishing that he had been clean for five years and calming me down, we both walked into the meeting late.

The swinging door creaked so loud that the speaker stopped sharing and the entire meeting turned its head to see who was walking in. The sweaty shame that set in for being late quickly dissipated when Rob giggled and waved at everyone, completely diffusing the situation, and we just kept walking until we got to the back of the room. He said it was better to sit back there because no one could hear you talk shit about them, and that was when I got my first true feeling that everything was going to be okay. I barely remember the meeting or what happened after. I do remember meeting Sasha, an angry little Jewish girl who talked more shit about people under her breath than Rob did. We became very close very fast.

The house would be dark by the time Rob dropped me off at the end of the night and empty when I woke up in the morning. Everyone in the house had a schedule to keep but me. I just needed to stay off drugs and go to meetings. The only real job I had to worry about was cleaning up after myself and occasionally taking the garbage out. But being newly sober, both of those tasks were daunting as fuck most of the time.

Every morning I would wake up, make a cup of coffee, and go downstairs to my mom's office where I would sit in front of the computer in a "Tattoos & Piercings" chat room for the entire fucking day chain-smoking Virginia Slim Light 120's that she used to hide in the bottom left drawer under the envelopes. I sat there for hours trying to get girls to show me their tits while I rubbed my balls through the hole in my boxers the entire time.

Back then the only weapon of seduction you had was a keyboard. There were no picture phones to send your chiseled torso through, nor could you get any pics in return. There was no way to tell if the person you were talking to was even the gender they were specifying. And on the slight chance that they did send you a picture, it would take at least forty-five minutes to download. It was faster to cook a TV dinner in a conventional oven than it was to jerk off to a girl's picture on the internet in the nineties. You fucking millennials don't know how goddamn easy you have it these days.

With the shades drawn and one of those long-ass cigarettes burning alone in the ashtray I would firmly grip my quivering manhood like a science monkey trapped in a cage with a drip bottle full of cocaine water. I had been opiated for so many years that the feeling of my dick actually getting hard in my hand was like losing my virginity all over again. I almost woke the entire rehab up the first time I came in the shower. Sasha was the one who turned me on to that chat room and we would sit in the private message box and talk shit about everyone else all day just like we did in meetings. My mother wasn't really stressing on me getting a job; she was just glad that I was staying clean and going to meetings. So to be a grateful son, I would empty the ashtray and get off the computer before she came home from work so it didn't look like all I was doing was chain-smoking and cumming in her office all day.

It was a big house with two floors so there was plenty of space to not be in the way...I hadn't lived with my family in years, so it was a bit of an adjustment for everyone. They put me in the bedroom that Nani slept in before she passed away, which meant that every time I jerked off I would think that she was watching, and that was a total bummer, plus the bed was really noisy so I couldn't get down like I wanted to. Other than that, it wasn't bad living there at all. It was definitely way worse before I got there.

Rob would pick me up every night around the same time everyone was getting home from work. We would drive down to Nyack for a meeting, and afterward people from both fellowships would meet up at the coffee shop down the street and order giant glasses of iced espresso coated with chocolate syrup and topped with whip cream. There was absolutely nothing recovery oriented about this drink because every time I had one, my left eye would start twitching and I would get really sweaty and quiet. I may as well have been shooting coke.

We would smoke cigarettes and talk shit all night, laughing so hard at their crazy drugged up adventures, and it was always a bummer when it was time to go home. These are the people who taught me not to be ashamed of being clean. Rob and all his friends made it feel totally normal to be a recovering drug addict. In New Jersey, all those lonely angry assholes ever talked about was "People, Places, and Things." They would say shit like, "If you hang out in a barber shop long enough, you're gonna get a haircut..." and whenever we would go into a diner there would always be that one dude who would take all the placemats off the table because they had drink recipes on them, and hand them to the waitress saying, "We're not gonna need these, honey, none of us drink." Everyone would chuckle and nod like they were so fucking special, and I remember feeling so embarrassed by that, and by them... How the fuck was I supposed to stay clean if I didn't want to be anything like the losers who were training me to be just like them?

It wasn't the heroin, my dad leaving, or the fact that I never wanted to grow up. No, I was deathly afraid of ending up like these sorry sack nobodies. I felt like I would have been better off being a junky. I always felt like I had more to offer than just mowing a lawn or making an Italian hero.

It was different with Rob and them. Instead of fearing people, places, and things, we laughed in the face of that despair. We would go see bands play at local bars and do shots of water, make out with drunk girls, go see concerts, and dance all night. These guys were young and all of them had five to fifteen years clean. No one here was getting a fucking haircut, and I wanted what they had.

Rob and I had both lived in California and wanted to be rock stars at some point in our lives and quickly formed a tight bond over being thrown back into the winter tundras and mosquito-infested summers of upstate New York trying to figure out our lives. It was no mistake that I was drawn to his car that cold and rainy night. We were meant to meet and figure it out together. Rob is one of those people that I had already known for years in another life, real kindred spirits type shit, and since everyone knew and loved him, I was automatically accepted into their group. I was lucky. A lot of people show up at an anonymous program and wander around aimlessly for years without ever finding a solid crew to stay warm under the wing of. I literally went from being a junky scumbag loser to this fun-loving dude running around Nyack like a crazy person. There were always acoustic guitars around, and Rob and I would play all the cheesy shit to get girls' attention. It was the nineties, so it was mostly rock and grungy type shit. I can still drop the fuck out of some panties with "Badfish" and "She Talks to Angels."

LADIES' NIGHT

THERE WERE THREE SEMI-HOT girls in NA, and within a month's time, I had slept with all of them. I even slept with Sasha sometimes, but our friendship was strong and it didn't affect us. I ghosted one girl, knocked up the other, and made her best friend my girlfriend because she had a car. The one I knocked up was an Irish Catholic of the severest descent and didn't know if she wanted to keep the baby or not for what turned out to be an agonizing couple of weeks. Almost overnight I went from being a fun-loving newcomer guy to the guy everyone quietly shook their heads at when I walked into the room. I had to hide in the back of meetings if I even showed up at all. I never intentionally set out to hurt anyone, I just had no life skills, or any way to cope with these newfound situations like an adult.

I had nine months clean and I wanted to kill myself. WHAT THE FUCK WAS HAPPENING!?!?!?! I would walk into a meeting and the heat streaming from the eyes of all the females in the room would literally burn right through my soul. I'd sweat bullets at every meeting I went to until I eventually just stopped showing up all together.

Part of the deal with me not doing my full sentence was that I had to complete five years of felony probation, which I had to start near Woodstock until they switched it to Rockland County. Mom and Rick had to work and couldn't take me up there, so I took the bus up a couple of days early to see Scott and Kelly and show everyone how good I was doing—and with nine months clean, I confidently stepped into the cold empty darkness of the Woodstock winter where I had no idea that the baron shadows of misery had been waiting patiently for me.

I couldn't really see straight; my thoughts were all jumbled, making my eyes foggy. My spirit was dark and alone, and I knew that I would be comforted the way I needed to be when I got there. All I needed was some fresh Woodstock air and some good conversation with the old homies to reset my brain and bring me back to a reality that I honestly couldn't get where I was.

The bus let me off in the center of town on the green. I used to take it up from Jersey all the time when I was a kid and the party would start as soon as I stepped onto the pavement. This time it was cold, dark, and the only person in sight was my friend Ian, who was working behind the counter at Ted's Corner Cupboard, the local deli that had been tending to our drunken stoner needs since before you were born. I never called anyone to tell them I was coming, I was just going to show up and surprise them, but on the way down the hill to call Scotty to come get me I saw the light on at my friends Purdy and Christine's place. This was the same place that I went to get stoned and meditate with the old roommate before that very first Beast show at Tinker Street Cafe in '94. They lived in the apartment right below where that old spot was, so I figured a stop in to say hello and see how they were doing wouldn't be that big of a deal.

It was cozy warm inside and smelled like some kind of cinnamon candle and weed, while Manson's *Antichrist Superstar* darkened the air in the house. I just caught them as they were leaving for Ladies' Night at The Joyous Lake. I sat on the couch and warmed my hands over the candle as the snow melted into the cuff of my Dickies. After hanging out for a few minutes and catching up with the old gang, I decided that I was just going to hang out with them for the night and head to Scott and Kelly's in the morning. It was Wednesday and I didn't have to be at probation until Friday morning, so I had some time to hang out.

Women drank free on ladies' night, so as a goof Purdy and I dressed up as girls with full makeup, dresses, and some high heels. I had absolutely no intention of drinking—I couldn't, or I would go to prison. I was just going to hang with my old friends and try to find that connection to my life I had been so desperately looking to find in Nyack.

Purdy opened the door to the bar and let me walk past him. The smell hit me as it usually does in that town and my shields dropped. I walked right up to the bar with everyone and ordered a seltzer, still confident I wasn't going to drink, but literally two sips in I turned to the bartender and ordered a Jack and Coke. Before I knew what was actually happening, I found myself slamming shots and doing coke in the little private room that looked over the stage while trying to convince Christine, who was a super lesbian, to make out with me. I thought I almost had her.

I spent the next day on their couch wrapped up in the worst Marilyn Manson hangover, quietly freaking out to myself about probation. I was so hungover I couldn't move. I had at least another day before I had to go in, so it was possible that I would test negative if I drank enough water. I still hadn't called Scott, Kelly, or anyone else who would have been conducive to my situation. The sun went down and I started to feel a lot better, and since I had probation at seven thirty the next morning, there was no fucking way I was drinking tonight. Only a complete moron would be so stupid as to do something that dangerous to their future...

I looked at the time and it was six in the morning, and there I was all coked up and drunk at Purdy's. I now had to rush to Kingston reeking of booze with a little bit of cocaine in my pocket. I was now completely fucked. I was just gonna walk in there and hope for the best, but I knew I was going to have to do the full six years or whatever the fuck it was. I stood out front smoking my last cigarette as a free man, dreading going up the stairs. Finally, I walked through the door with my fate sealed in my aching head, eventually being brought into a tiny office with a woman sitting across from me. I couldn't stop staring at the specimen cup sitting next to her on the desk. The office was so small, I was afraid to breathe petrified that she would smell me. A man younger than I, wearing a button-down pastel shirt, grabbed the cup and walked me into the bathroom, where he stood directly in front of me staring at my trembling hands trying to keep my shriveled up coke dick inside this tiny plastic cup. The bright yellow piss filled quickly to the top as I let the rest stream into the toilet. I capped it up and handed it back. The cup was placed on a brown tray and put back on the desk. The PO drew a couple of dipsticks out of the drawer and put them into the cup at the same time. She said that they were only told to check for opiates, which I didn't do. The sticks all turned green, and I was free to go.

THE NEWCOMER

I WENT BACK TO Purdy's just to get it out of my system for one more night then straight back home to stand up as a newcomer the next day. After the meeting, I waited for everyone to come at me with hugs and pats on the back followed by the ever so popular yet completely condescending, "Keep coming back" that I got from just about every meeting I ever went back to after a relapse. I got that at this meeting as well, but not from Rob and the other guys. They didn't say anything to me. They all just left, except for Sasha. She stuck by me through the whole thing. I called Rob confused when I got home to see what was up and was completely blown away when he said, "Call me when you get six months, and then maybe we can talk."

What in the actual fuck??? I was a fucking newcomer! THE MOST IMPORTANT PERSON IN THE ROOM! That's what those fucking assholes always said in their shares. How could he do this to me? Thank God that the girl with the kid was still willing to hang out with me and drive me around, so now I had Sasha and the girl with the kid and the car to hang out with. My circle had become extremely small.

I wanted to get sober again, I really did. Those few days upstate were fun but also miserably exhausting, and I couldn't fathom losing what I had just built for myself at my mom's. I was so pissed at Rob because I really needed him and I felt like he totally bailed on me. The other guys were still cordial but withdrawn because they were afraid I was going to die. I wouldn't understand that concept until much later, so for now I would just stay pissed.

I had to go to a mandated outpatient program five days a week from nine to three. I would take a six a.m. bus to get there in time just so I could sit in a circle with the biggest losers in Rockland County and pretend to care. One of the biggest fucking wastes of time in the world are county-run mental health facilities. The counselors are useless and have no idea how to help anyone, and all that I got out of that program was this boring little paragraph for the book. I hadn't even thought about that place once until now because there was absolutely no use for what they had in my life ever.

My "girlfriend" would pick me up at three and take me to her mom's house, where I would sit on the living room floor with her two-year-old daughter watching *Teletubbies* until a sandwich magically appeared in my lap. Her mom would come home from work around five and sneer at me until we left for a meeting.

I got the one giant Black preacher guy in NA to sponsor me, and the first thing he told me to do was get a commitment. Something that would make sure that I went to the same meeting every week. If I didn't want to go, too bad. I had to because now I had this fucking commitment and people were relying on me, and if I went to the same meeting every week people would get to know me. It was also supposed to give me a sense of purpose in life, which I didn't really understand but whatever, getting loaded wasn't an option anymore so I had to do whatever they told me to do. There were a few to choose from. I could greet people as they came in the door (fuck that), I could make the sponsorship announcement at the end of the meeting (boring), or I could make the coffee—perfect. I fucking loved coffee, and all these people were now gonna love mine. I didn't understand how making coffee at an NA meeting was going to keep me off of heroin, I just knew that I had to do whatever they told me to do. That was the deal.

When I moved back to Mom's, I got on welfare, so I was able to pay for the coffee and all the fixin's with food stamps. I had the girlfriend take me to the store then drop me off at the meeting, where I put all the stuff onto a long folding table in the back of the room. I dumped the entire can of coffee into the top of this old dented industrial coffee pot, flipped on the switch, and started laying out the treats.

One thing I noticed immediately when I started going to meetings was the lack of care for the coffee commitment. Sometimes there was nothing but a package of stale chocolate chip cookies from the dollar store sitting next to a container of unflavored powdered creamer. I always thought that they should be exiled for that shit, because it really is the most important commitment.

I was also super nervous and wanted people to like me back then, so I bought my favorite Entenmann's cakes and symmetrically placed cut pieces onto a kaleidoscope arrangement of paper doilies. I brought real half-and-half, *and* flavored creamer, raw sugar, and plenty of cups stacked evenly next to everything. After I set the whole thing up, I went and stood in the corner and anxiously waited for people to start showing up. As they came in, I could see the surprise on their face when they saw the display I had laid out. It was exactly the reaction I was hoping for, like they'd just walked into a free wedding buffet and not some shitty NA meeting. To some of these people a meeting is all they had. It was all I fucking had, anyway, so I figured if I could give some hopeless junky a little bit of joy at the end of his crappy day my service was fulfilled.

At the end of the meeting, everyone got in a circle to do the serenity prayer, and right before the secretary said, "Let's all thank Jason for making a great pot of coffee and bringing such wonderful snacks." After the meeting everyone thanked me like I was the only coke dealer at the party and told me how they wished I did the coffee at every meeting. Now I understood how getting a coffee commitment could help keep someone sober. I had a sense of purpose that I never had before. Something else also happened, the guy who collected the money for the meeting came up to me and asked if I had a receipt from my purchase. Confused, I handed him the little piece of paper from my pocket, and he handed me a bunch of cash in return. I wasn't even thinking about getting reimbursed, and now I had twenty dollars cash in my hand! I got as many coffee commitments as I could and made my poor girlfriend put all the coffee pots in her trunk and clank them around to every meeting we went to. I was making at least a hundred bucks a week off of Narcotics Anonymous for months.

I tried to hang out in NA as long as I could, but it was tainted now. I no longer wanted to have sex with the girl that was driving me around. I sure as fuck didn't want to be someone's stepfather, and all her friends still looked at me like I was Ted Bundy anyway, so fuck it I was out. But the final straw for this fellowship of sorts was that it was always the same twenty-five people bitching about the same middle-class white people shit night after night. I didn't want to be anything like these people. Luckily for me Alcoholics Anonymous had meetings in the exact same places NA did, so it was easy for me to just wait an extra hour and go hide in the other fellowship. The first thing I noticed when I got there was that everyone seemed way calmer. They were showered, smelled nice, and dressed like they might have some shit going on, and didn't sound like they just got out of prison. It was a welcomed switch.

As promised, when I got six months, Rob and the guys started talking to me again, and I was back sitting in the front of Starbucks for the post- and pre-meeting hangs like nothing ever happened. It was nice to finally belong somewhere again; I was roaming around alone and miserable for what felt like a fucking lifetime.

I was coming up on two years sober and finally moved out of my mom's and into a very tiny room at this sober house in Nyack. Mom and Rick broke up (again), and she got a new mechanic boyfriend who helped me get a little car to tool around town in.

I absolutely loved living in Nyack. There was always someone from the meetings either working or hanging around wherever I was, and I loved that, but it was also time for me to start spreading my wings if I wanted to resurrect any sort of dream that had previously died in my soul. I didn't want to end up some chain-smoking old schmuck stuck at a shitty job, renting a tiny room in someone else's house, sharing in every noon meeting just so I could hear myself talk. I've seen that guy way too often over the years, and he has literally chased me out of recovery numerous times. I started driving up to Woodstock on the weekends to visit the old homies and break up the monotony of everyday AA life in Nyack.

I was sober and happy, so there was no longer any girl or junky drama. I had never been comfortable being comfortable, which meant there was only one other way for me to experience a good dose of pain without destroying my life completely. I stopped into the local tattoo shop just outside of town and had some dude I didn't even know start a dragon sleeve on my left arm. This would represent balance, wisdom, and serenity—how appropriate. After a couple of visits, I became friends with the piercer and decided it was time to get my dick pierced.

It truly seemed like a fantastic idea at the time.

PRINCE ALBERT

THE DAY I WENT UP to get my Prince Albert, I stopped in town to get a sandwich because no one should ever get their dick stabbed on an empty stomach. I randomly bumped into Tony and asked if he wouldn't mind holding my hand during this process. He agreed, and together we skipped down the hill.

The smell of ointment and rubbing alcohol made my anxious stomach dizzy while the outlaw country playing in the background made me feel a little tougher than I did before I walked through the door. The girl who was about to prick my prick was the girlfriend of the guy doing my sleeve. Her apprentice was a very butch lesbian with a cop haircut, and I am only assuming she was a lesbian because she looked like one of my father's sisters and had a shirt on that said "We Don't Need Balls To Play." I was to get a discount if I let her help out during the process, which I agreed to since I was always broke and willing to give someone new a chance to touch my dick.

I dropped my pants and boxers to my ankles and hopped my ass up onto the cold vinyl table, resting my elbows behind me while the breeze cooled my nervous balls and my dick sat flaccid against my right inner thigh. The piercer approached me with the biggest needle I had ever seen in my life while the apprentice crept up behind her holding a metal tube the size of a cigarette. The look on Tony's face was confusion and fear, asking me why I was doing this as the blood slowly fell from his face to his stomach. I was too dumb to have any idea what I had actually signed up for and was way too busy trying to impress girls I wasn't attracted to anyway.

The procedure was simple, you put the tube in the head of the dick, stick the needle through the foreskin under the head until it comes out of the tube, follow it with the ring and poof...all done.

Easy peasy, lemon squeezy. Right?

Wrong.

The lesbian asked if she could touch my penis to insert the tube. I jokingly asked when the last time she touched one in real life was, and she was not into the side commentary at all. Note to everyone: Don't ever test a butch lesbian's manhood while she's got your penis in her hand.

Tony grabbed my free hand, I took the deepest breath I could, and we both watched the piercer take that giant fishhook and force it into the undercarriage of my shriveled little dickhead. A tear formed in Tony's left eye when the skin broke and we both heard the cartilage ripping. I thought it was over, but something wasn't right, the needle was dangling from my dick and I heard the tube bounce onto the floor. The apprentice choked and let go of the tube too early and it popped out before she could get the ring in. The piercer asked nervously if we wouldn't mind doing it again. I didn't feel Tony's hand anymore, because he was now on one knee with his hand over his mouth.

She pulled the needle out, and now there was blood trickling down my fingers as I gently tried to comfort my scared little weenus. The apprentice grabbed a new tube and reinserted it, by which time Tony was out of the room and maybe out of the building altogether. The piercer once again came with the needle and BOOM, the fucking apprentice choked again. The piercer looked at me, shaking her head no with the fear of God in her eyes as the tube rolled underneath the table, and I told her to just push the needle through anyway. As she tried to pull the needle out and cancel the whole transaction, I grabbed her hand and forced it, pushing it through myself.

I thought the cartilage ripped before! Whoooooo doggy…

Blood was now all over my crotch, the floor, and her gloved hand as she rushed to grab the ring and slide it through. I laid all the way back, resting my head against the wall as blood, sweat, and tears, streamed down from every which way. She slipped the ring in through the bottom, but it was not going through the tip. She said there was no way we could go through with this anymore, and I should just let all this heal and come back at a later date.

I sat up, I saw red, and I grabbed her hand once again and pushed it until I heard a pop. She looked at me and told me that I was the toughest dude they had ever seen and slid a condom on to catch all the blood. I didn't need the outlaw country to make me feel like a man anymore, for I had this incompetent lesbian to help me overcome my insecurities. I pulled up my pants, obviously didn't have to pay, and went back to Mom's to lie down and cry for a few hours.

I was given a few rules before I left the tattoo parlor:

1. Keep the area extremely clean

2. Pee sitting down

3. And NO SEX with anyone, even myself, for at least two weeks

Which all sounded easy enough, until I had to go to the store and get cigarettes. I took Mom's keys and jumped in the car, heading down to Cumberland Farms. It was around nine p.m. and Woodstock turns into a ghost town after seven, so I was the only one on the road. As I parked the car and started toward the door, I noticed an extremely hot curly haired blonde girl whom I had never seen before pulling up to a gas pump, an extremely rare sight in these parts. Another rare thing that happened was she was staring at me like I was a steak and she was a dog that hadn't eaten in days.

I went in, bought smokes, and held the door for her as she was coming in. I got in the car and waited for her to pay and come back out—and she was still clocking me like fuck as she got back into her car. As she started to pull away I rolled down my window to get her attention and asked her if she wanted to hang out, which she obviously obliged. This has never happened to me in my fucking life let alone in the middle of nowhere at this time of night. She followed me back to my mom's and we snuck downstairs into the bedroom. The house was old and hollow and you could fucking hear everything from wherever you were standing in it.

I tried to explain my situation but she was literally all over me. I was so fucking turned on and in so much pain that I really didn't know my ass from my elbow anymore. I went to the bathroom and unzipped the condom in the toilet. I was so turned on that all the blood that rushed through the head almost filled the condom completely. I came back out with my dick swinging between my legs to show her what I had done that day, and she immediately put her mouth on it. I held in the scream from the unbearable euphoria I was now feeling, grabbed her by her ears, and threw her on the bed ripping all her clothes off in what felt like one smooth motion.

I ate her pussy for as long as I could, trying to get the heartbeat of my dick to calm down some, but I was too excited. I grabbed her legs and pushed them as far away from one another as I could, extra slowly sliding the head of my wounded dick inside her. She was so tight I started to see spots and my body convulsed as razor blades shot out of my dick. I fucked her slow, slower than I'd ever fucked anyone in my entire life, and she came immediately from all the excitement, which also made me cum immediately. I had never felt a pain mixed with euphoria like this all at one time.

We were having such an intense moment that I didn't even hear my mother come down the stairs. She opened the door screaming as I stood there dripping blood and cum all over one of Grandma Angela's antique rugs while this poor girl got her clothes together and ran out of the house.

I didn't even get her name.

NO HOPE

I WAS AT THE Bergen Pines NA meeting in Jersey, sitting in the dark circle of heavily dentured arrogance minding my own business, when the electric doors gently swung open and she came in and sat down. I couldn't take my fucking eyes off of her. She shared that her name was Elaina and how she wished she could rip up her needle exchange card and stop shooting dope. She was the closest thing to an obsession I'd had since Colleen Rausch in fifth grade (who actually became my cousin through marriage in later years). I never cared enough about girls to be obsessed like that and it definitely threw me off my game, but I was also too nervous to talk to her after the meeting, and she vanished through the cloud of cigarette smoke in the parking lot. I must have made Aunt Marie drive me to at least three meetings a day for the next two weeks looking for this girl, but I never saw her again.

I think it's good to have a nice unhealthy obsession with someone, especially when you're a newcomer. It's good to have someone or something that makes you want to go to those boring ass meetings every day. So when I found Hope, she was all I needed to get through my first year in this new fellowship. The first time I saw her in front of the church she looked up at me and said, "What the fuck are you doing here?" almost like she knew me. She spit on the ground as she squashed a lit cigarette butt with her Doc Marten and walked into the meeting before I could give her my answer. I immediately fell in love, and for at least three months I left flowers on her porch, notes on her car windshield outside of meetings, and constantly pestered her to go out with me. I lost sleep night after night over this girl I didn't even know, lying there thinking about what she was doing, hoping she would be at every meeting. And when she wasn't, I wondered where she was and who she was with. I made myself absolutely crazy. The whole time I was doing this, she was obsessed with some other dude who wanted nothing to do with her, so at least we had one thing in common.

I painted my room a deep red with dark purple trim and put a giant poster of Jimi Hendrix's head on the wall right in front of my futon so that every time I woke up and jerked off, Jimi was watching. I had a dresser and a TV with a VCR that came with the room, a borrowed four track, and a bunch of incense and candles that I stole from my mother. The room was so small that if I lit more than one candle at a time it would turn the place into a sauna, but it was my very first place that was mine alone, so I didn't care. True independence was a totally new feeling for me; I had no idea how much I needed it until I got it. I would sit in that room for days, chain-smoking Marlboro Reds out the window in front of the stereo, learning how to play Mazzy Star and Lenny Kravitz songs on my shitty little acoustic, and hoping to impress Hope later that night in front of the coffee house. I was madly obsessed and needed to be near her constantly. I would do anything to stare at those big brown eyes and perfect lips. I'd sit on the street corners of Central Nyack with Rob and a bunch of other people after meetings singing shitty Sublime songs and one-hit wonders from the nineties then go home alone while I wondered why she wouldn't kiss me, and she wondered where Angelo, the guy who didn't want to be with her, was.

Alcoholics love to self-torture.

I was always worried that once I stopped drinking and doing drugs my life would be over. I was not aware that I never actually had a life worth losing and that I would be having the most gut-wrenching, laugh-until-you-pee fun I ever had in my life once I got sober. When we weren't making fun of people outside of Starbucks or talking shit in a meeting, we would drive over to Manhattan to get food, maybe see a comedy show, and hit on the sober girls at the midnight meeting on Varick and Houston.

THE FREEDOM OF OZZFEST

OZZFEST '99 WAS THE first time I found out that I could actually go into an active setting, have an amazing time, and not get loaded. I was so brainwashed by those fucking NA dudes in Jersey that I thought I could never be around places where there were drugs and alcohol ever again. Rob and those guys showed me a different way, a better way. We all carpooled to the PNC Arts Center for the day but stopped at the coffee shop for one of those crackhead espressos. The caffeine kicked in a little way down the road and the car got so quiet you would have thought we were all shooting coke. I remember our friend Erik (by far the funniest motherfucker in the group) leaning his head against the passenger seat window as he looked quietly into the distance, finally opening his mouth and breaking the ice by saying, "I feel really weird, man..." which burst us all out into a fit of laughter, and that was all it took to make everything okay. We were all feeling it, but sometimes it just takes someone to say that shit out loud to defuse what might be an embarrassing situation.

I was honestly a little nervous going there. I knew that everyone would be drunk and it was my first sober concert and blah blah blah, but I was with my crew so I knew I would be looked after. That day I found out who System of a Down were, watched

Slayer play during the day (which was weird and a first for me), and embarrassed myself in front of Evan Seinfeld and his friends. But the topper was watching Slipknot. The band was completely insane, and their fans were even crazier. Poor Fear Factory had to play after them and I don't even think anyone stuck around to see them, especially since Sabbath was headlining the main stage at the same time. The best part of the night was dancing like a fucking hippy without a care in the world to Black Sabbath at the far edge of the lawn, away from all the drunk idiots. I kept picking up half empty cups of beer off the ground and holding them up over my head pretending I was hammered while screaming "OOOOOOZZZZYYYYYYYYYYY!!!!!!!" and the drunk idiots would yell back. We were laughing so hard.

I owe all those fucking dudes my life just from that one day alone.

THE FINAL DAYS

I GOT BORED AND quit the autobody place, eventually getting a job as a catering waiter at a banquet hall in Nyack. That was absolutely grueling, and although I really needed money and the chicken marsala shift meal was bomb as fuck, I just couldn't handle it. I kept dropping trays full of food and sweating too much in that tuxedo shit I had to wear so I just bounced. Rob got me a job at the recycling place he and our friend Johnny worked at, which meant I now had to wake up at four a.m. and ride around Rockland County dumping bins full of wet newspaper and juicy cat food cans into our pseudo garbage trucks. I was only at that job for about two weeks before I noticed how ripped I was getting. I loved catching the lonely housewives peering through the living room curtains while they masturbated through their robes as we bounced from lawn to lawn sweating and shirtless. But that job also sucked sweaty hamster balls, so after about a month of that bullshit, when Rob came knocking on my bedroom door to wake me up like he did every morning, I told him to go fuck himself and that I was never going back. Regular people employment has never really been my thing.

I woke up around noon that day and went to Starbucks to stare at girls and wait for someone to give me a really cool job. I know you're thinking "Who the fuck does that?" Well, I do, and it works most of the time.

Here, I'll show you…

My buddy Dylan showed up and sat with me. He was in AA but never worked any steps or had a sponsor. He didn't do any of the shit they wanted you to do to be a part of their little cult. He would come to meetings and hang out in the back with us and laugh. I always looked up to him because he was ten years sober and everyone always said that you couldn't stay sober unless you did the things, but Dylan was the unicorn in AA who told them all to go fuck themselves in the sweetest way possible, and I loved that.

I told him I had just quit that shit job with Rob and Johnny and he laughed, asking me if I would want to try being a production assistant. He was an assistant director on feature films. I had no idea what that meant, but I decided to take him up on his offer. When I said yes he was literally like, "Cool, man, be at my house at five tomorrow morning."

Just like that!

Luckily I was used to getting up at an ungodly hour from that shit job and met him at his big yellow house near the water. He had the same old-school espresso percolator that my Nani used to have. I stood in his kitchen tiredly sipping the hot bean water, excited for my new adventure and hoping that I wouldn't have to do any actual work.

Dylan had a holder in his car for a cell phone. I didn't even have a landline in my room let alone a cell phone; I had to use the house phone all the way downstairs in the living room. This guy was super big time. The thing I liked most about Dylan was that he talked to me like I was a person and not some moron that was brand new in AA. Even though I had two and a half years sober, people still talked to me like I was a child. I have always had a massive problem with condescending attitudes from most people who are supposedly "saving you." Even though I had no idea what I was doing, he treated me with respect and was very patient with me. Thank you for that, my man.

BRAVO/PRODUCTION

W<small>E DROVE TO THE</small> corner of Central Park South and Fifth Avenue—Grand Army Plaza. It was still dark when we got there, but I vividly remember a statue of a man riding a golden stallion glowing in the headlights as we pulled up. Dylan told me to get out and grab a radio from the production trailer. I didn't know what a production trailer was or what he meant by a radio. All he did was point in a general direction, so instead of asking him what he meant I just started banging on trucks asking everyone where the radios were, pissing off all the early morning crankholes in the electric and grip departments. I eventually walked up on this dude sitting on the trailer steps in a sleeveless basketball jersey holding a radio in one hand and a lit cigarette in the other, looking at me like I was about to annoy him just like the other assholes. Turns out he was actually in charge of the walkie-talkies (what Dylan meant when he said radio). He walked me over to his little black box and showed me how to put it on and use it. Much to my surprise he was actually super cool and helpful, and he quickly became my production *hermano*.

It was an immediate friendship, one of those "brothers in another life"–type things. He took me under his wing and taught me how to be a jaded PA immediately. His name was Tom, but everyone was calling him Johnny Bravo because he looked just like the cartoon character. You can find Bravo playing the bike messenger, singing "Sara Smiles" by Hall and Oates somewhere in the middle of that movie.

This was the funnest job I'd ever had. I got to stand on a street corner a mile away from the actual set for about eighteen hours screaming "CUT!" and "ROLLING!" whether anyone could hear me or not. I finally felt important, telling old people who had been walking a certain way to work their entire life that today they had to go a different way because John Cusack was making a mediocre rom-com. Also, this job was way harder than you would think. Turns out people get fucking mad when you disrupt their everyday routine. Little old men would yell shit in a foreign language and swat at me with folded newspapers; Asian ladies would smack me with their umbrellas as they walked right past me blasting into the shot, making the first AD lose his fucking mind in my earpiece. But I was really good at this job, and I totally enjoyed being a dick.

Dylan picked me up every morning at four unless it was a night shoot. I worked Monday through Friday, all day and night, and made a whopping ninety dollars per day, which was fine because you couldn't spend your money anyway because you worked so much. I was great at locking up a street corner and running really fast to get things that were needed on set, which is basically all you needed to do to keep your job. It was the first time I had an actual purpose in life other than making coffee for a bunch of old scumbags, and it kept me very busy. PAs are the first ones on set in the morning, and the last ones to leave at night, which was also the morning again. When I wasn't running around like a madman for the AD, I would use my time wisely by trying to seduce unknown actresses hoping to get their big break in the background holding area with my radio on my hip like I was actually in charge of shit. When we finished *Serendipity,*

Dylan asked me if I wanted to keep working. He said everyone liked me so he could get me on a bunch more stuff.

My next job was on *Riding in Cars With Boys*, which Bravo was on but not Dylan. So I stayed in the city with my grandmother (who had obviously forgiven me), and since they were filming upstate, we would meet a shuttle bus somewhere in the city and take it to wherever we were filming.

I ended up having to watch the inside of a flower shop in a town called Tuckahoe that was run by a mother and daughter, making sure no one came through the back door while they were filming in the front. Within the first two hours I had convinced the hot little daughter to sneak in the back room and make out with me the entire time they were filming. I definitely wasn't calling rolling and cut during those breaks. The next day Bravo and I were put in charge of the background actresses for the wedding scene. Whose bright idea was this?! After spending all day smoking cigarettes and watching these girls run around in their seventies-style bridesmaid dresses, I ended up having one of them meet me at my grandmother's apartment after work. If it was a night shoot I would get home after grandma had already left for work, so it was perfect. I sat next to her on the shuttle home, rubbing her leg under her jacket, which was conveniently placed on her lap. We all had been up for about twenty-eight hours by now and were fucking delirious. A twenty-eight-hour day in Tuckahoe, New York, just imagine that.

The next day when I got to work there was drama. She was bragging to her extra friends about how she hooked up with me, but one of the girls she was yapping to saw me kissing the flower girl the day before and told her. It was an uncomfortable day to say the least, but at least it made Bravo laugh his fucking ass off.

Grandma was over me staying there all the time again, so I eventually got a place in Washington Heights with my buddy

Austin from Nyack. Actually, Austin was the one who was supposed to do the sketches in the first book. That was our dream as sober young studs perusing through the nightlife of Rockland County, NY. He always loved my songwriting and said I should write a book about my life, and he would etch on the blank page at the beginning of each chapter. When I finally wrote the fucking thing, we had lost touch, and when I hit him up he didn't seem too stoked until he finally told me he couldn't do it because he didn't have time. But I love what Jonah did with everything and it was perfect, so it all worked out for the best, I guess.

Austin and I got a two-bedroom apartment on the first floor right on the corner of 178th and Fort Washington. Our backyard was the George Washington Bridge, which I thought was super cool. I always wanted to be one of those douchebags who moved to NYC and talked shit about Jersey like I didn't grow up there.

This was way before all the hot girls with little dogs moved into that area. The rent was so cheap I could have panhandled for it on the street if I needed. We were the only white guys for blocks and blocks. I actually had to learn a little Spanish just so I could order food. Mambi, around the corner on Broadway, sold fresh roasted chickens that splattered grease all over the front window with rice and beans and a Coke for three bucks and it would feed you for days. They also had the fucking absolute best café con leche ever. We were living like kings.

I met a hot singer girl in Greenwich Village AA, and she let me come jam with her band a few times in this basement on Ludlow and Houston, but unfortunately that was the extent of my music life other than jamming in my room to Sick of It All and Metallica CDs. It did spark that little fire inside me to start playing music with other people again, though. I really needed to get back to LA, man. It was getting cold again, and I didn't want to work for a living anymore.

THE GIRL ON THE TRAIN

A NOTHER INTERESTING MOVIE I WORKED on was *K-PAX*. I had no idea Kevin Spacey was gay until he started walking past me on set and making super uncomfortable whispery comments while eye fucking me behind his bodyguard. I made friends with Ajay Naidu and actually got him to do the dance flip that he did in *Office Space* while we were outside smoking a cigarette together. Then I got yelled at by the wardrobe lady for getting his long white coat all wrinkly and dirty.

I also took a liking to a background actress who shall remain nameless, because I can't remember her name, but I have been wondering about this red-haired green-eyed voluptuous vixen on and off for years. We spent all day filming the same ten second scene over and over on a commuter train. I was crouched down behind her seat and every time we started rolling I would whisper shit to try and make her laugh during the scene. This won her over, so much so that later in the morning when we wrapped she came and found me while I was watching the camera truck. She told me that she lived nearby and that I should come over when I was finished and take a nap with her, telling me that the number on the door was broken and hanging upside-down, and that she would leave it unlocked so that I could just come in. I couldn't believe how fucking easy she was making this. I must have been really funny.

It was starting to get light out, and I still had another hour or so before I could leave. Man, that was the longest hour of my fucking life. As soon as they told me I could, I made the mad dash for her place. It was winter, and I was decked out in about a thousand dollars' worth of navy blue North Face gear from head to toe with a scarf wrapped around my face and a wool hat pulled all the way over most of my eyes so the lids wouldn't freeze open. I finally found the building through all the crazy wind and snow and barged my way into the door, making my way up the narrow steps to the fourth floor. I think that's what she said anyway. I got to the second floor and saw 2B, with the letter hanging upside-down on the door, I tried the doorknob and it turned all the way, so I pushed my way in and there she was wrapped in a white comforter, glistening in the sunlight that was coming through the window. It was a tiny bachelor apartment. I remember a shoji screen with some clothes hanging off it right next to the door when I came in.

She started to rustle inside the blanket, and when she sat up I noticed that her hair was super curly, but on the train it was straight. I just figured she washed it when she got home or whatever, no big deal...Muffled, through my scarf, I said, "Baby, I'm here..." she opened her eyes after rubbing them, looked at me, and started screaming like she was getting stabbed in the stomach with a rusty bread knife. I kept saying, "Baby, it's me, Jason," but each time I said it the brick walls shook more from her screams getting louder.

I forgot that I still had the scarf and knit cap covering most of my face and looked like a mugging rapist. Eventually my eyes thawed out as I moved a little closer to the bed, which threw her into more of a panic. She was now tucked up in the corner of the mattress with her back against the brick screaming to save her life. This whole thing only lasted about thirty seconds, but it felt like an hour. My eyes finally dried up and I realized it wasn't her, and I was in the wrong apartment. It was a *number* that was supposed to be upside-down, not a fucking letter. And also I was two floors off.

My face got really hot and prickly, like that feeling you get when you're caught doing some shady shit you shouldn't be doing. I yelled "LOCK YOUR FUCKING DOOR, LADY!" and ran out of the apartment, but I didn't run out of the building. I was way too horny for that. I ran up two more flights of stairs listening to her screams echo down every hallway while I blew past all the opening doors as the curious neighbors came to see what was happening. I was so scared that they were going to start chasing me.

Fucking...terrifying...

I found the door with the hanging number and gently knocked even though it was open a little. I heard a soft voice say, "Come in," while the poor woman two floors down still shrieked through the halls. I couldn't close and lock that fucking door behind me fast enough. I was shaking, sweating, and petrified, but all that went away as soon as I walked in and saw this gorgeous naked woman lying under a blanket on a futon in the exact same layout as the apartment I was just in. I sat beside her catching my breath. She looked at me and said, "What is all that screaming?" I told her what happened as the sweat dripped down the center of my chest, hoping she wouldn't completely freak out, but she just laughed and started taking my clothes off, and yada yada yada, that was that. By far one of the most frightening moments immediately followed by the most intense sexual experiences I have ever had. I was so charged up from what had just happened I lasted about three minutes before sliding around her stomach in my own cum and passing out hard on her tits for a good six hours.

TIME MACHINE

PLAYING MUSIC WASN'T EVEN a pipe dream anymore. The bass and tiny practice amp in my room were all that was left of my silly little dream, and I would lie there at night thinking about never playing music with a band again and that scared the fuck out of me. But then the alarm clock would ring and it was time to run to a train and go to work.

I had become comfortable with a steady paycheck no matter how shitty it was and just immersed myself into work and sobriety to forget about the thought of ever going to California again, even in the dead of winter. I even stopped making my own music on the four track and dreaming of what Third & Bonnie Brae smelled like.

I got a call to work on *Time Machine*, a remake of the classic to be directed by H. G. Wells' great grandson. They were flying a crew in from Los Angeles and the PAs would be the only local crew. We were warned that they do things a little differently out there so an adjustment would most likely have to be made to our attitudes, but I didn't give a fuck. Just tell me what corner to stand on and no one will penetrate my fortress while you're filming.

We were a week into filming the movie and were now up in Albany, where I was standing on a frozen lake for fourteen hours hating everything about my existence and questioning every life choice I had ever made. Right at the moment when I was thinking about quitting everything like I usually do, Tommy, the second AD, walked over and asked if I wanted to come out to LA and finish the movie with them. All I would have to do was find a place to stay and they would fly me out, which would also give me work for at least the next three months in fucking Los Angeles.

I took it as an immediate sign from the Great Spirit and didn't give Tommy a chance to blink before I said yes. I went home early the next morning and told Austin that I would be leaving for a few months for work. He looked at me and said, "You're never coming back."

I got on a plane the next day headed to Venice to stay with Lari, Shala, and Allison one more time while I worked on this movie.

I was totally planning on going back to New York when the job was done…